STRATEGIES FOR A

Better

LIFE

A JOURNEY TO FINANCIAL EMPOWERMENT

ROSE PARKER JOHNSON

BAYMAR PUBLISHING

Published in Canada

ISBN 978-1-998753-31-4 (ebook)
ISBN 978-1-998753-32-1 (paperback)
ISBN 978-1-998753-33-8 (audio)

The information provided in this book is for educational purposes only. It is not intended to be a source of financial or legal advice. Making adjustments to a financial strategy or plan should only be undertaken after consulting with a professional. The publisher and the author make no guarantee of financial results obtained by using this book.

For questions and comments about this book, contact us at books@baymarpublishing.com.
Visit www.baymarpublishing.com

CONTENTS

INTRODUCTION

This book serves as a comprehensive guide to navigating the complexities of personal finance, equipping readers with the knowledge, tools, and strategies necessary to take control of their financial futures.

Imagine standing at the helm of your financial ship, steering towards a destination of prosperity and abundance. Here, we will explore the advantages of financial empowerment, uncovering the opportunities that await those who seize control of their financial destinies. For a complete picture, we will also cover the potential pitfalls, ensuring that you're equipped to overcome any challenges that may arise.

Before setting sail towards your financial goals, it is essential to lay down a sturdy foundation to build on. We will begin by evaluating your present financial situation, creating a clear snapshot of your assets, liabilities, and overall financial health. With this newfound clarity, you will be better equipped to chart a course toward your desired destination with confidence and purpose.

With your financial foundation in place, it will be time to set sail towards the horizon of your aspirations. Together, we will examine the art of goal setting, enabling you to successfully navigate the ocean of uncertainty by prioritizing your goals based on their importance and urgency.

You will encounter challenges and obstacles along the way. From managing debt to building and maintaining good credit, we will equip you with the tools and strategies necessary to navigate these waters with grace and resilience. By cultivating a disciplined approach to spending, saving, and investing, you will emerge stronger and more resilient than ever before.

Life is unpredictable, and financial storms can arise when least expected. That is why it is crucial to maintain an emergency fund—a financial safety net designed to cushion the impact of unexpected expenses. By building and maintaining this fund, you will fortify your defenses against the uncertainties of tomorrow and weather any storm that comes your way.

It is essential to explore new avenues for income generation and wealth accumulation. From passive income opportunities to investment strategies such as real estate and dividend stocks, we will unlock new pathways towards prosperity and abundance. To optimize your earning potential and safeguard your financial future, it is advisable to diversify your revenue streams.

It is also important to keep your sights set on the horizon of long-term wealth preservation. From estate planning to retirement strategies, we will equip you with the tools necessary to safeguard your legacy and secure your golden years. By adopting a proactive approach to wealth preservation, you will lay the groundwork for a future defined by security, stability, and peace of mind.

Technology is a valuable ally in the quest for financial success. We will look at ways to use new tools and technologies to improve your financial path, from investment platforms to cryptocurrencies and block-chain technology. You will have a competitive advantage in the always-changing field of personal finance if you embrace innovation and stay on top of it.

Personal branding has emerged as a key driver of professional success. From establishing an online presence to networking effectively for career growth, we will explore how you can build a compelling personal brand that showcases your unique talents and expertise. By positioning yourself as a thought leader in your field, you will open up new opportunities for career advancement and financial success.

Negotiation is a skill that can yield substantial dividends in both your personal and professional life.

From negotiating salary and benefits to navigating business deals and contracts, we will explore strategies for mastering the delicate art of persuasion and compromise. By honing your negotiation skills, you will unlock new avenues for financial gain and career advancement.

At the heart of financial empowerment lies a fundamental shift in mindset from scarcity to abundance, from fear to confidence. We will explore techniques for overcoming limiting beliefs and cultivating a positive and abundant mindset that attracts wealth and success. By embracing a mindset of abundance, you will open yourself up to a world of limitless potential and untold opportunity.

As you ascend the ladder of financial success, it is essential to strive for excellence and innovation continuously. We will explore advanced wealth-building strategies, such as legacy building, and the importance of consistent financial habits and routines. By embracing a philosophy of lifelong learning and growth, you will cultivate the habits and behaviors necessary to build and preserve wealth sustainably for generations to come.

1

TAKING CONTROL OF
YOUR FINANCIAL FUTURE

John and Jane are a middle-class family who want to improve their financial situation. Jane heard the term financial empowerment from one of her friends in yoga class. John asked her what financial empowerment is, but Jane is at a loss for words. What is Financial Empowerment?

The process of taking charge of one's finances, creating a sense of security, and developing the capacity to make wise financial decisions is referred to as financial empowerment. It encompasses more than just maintaining financial stability. It also entails providing people with the information, abilities, and tools needed to negotiate the challenging terrain of personal finance successfully.

At its core, financial empowerment encompasses various elements, including financial literacy, budgeting, saving, investing, and planning for the future. It is about more than just accumulating wealth. It emphasizes the development of a holistic and sustainable financial mindset. Individuals who are financially empowered not only understand the fundamentals of managing money but also have the confidence to apply this knowledge in their day-to-day lives.

Financial empowerment is not merely a luxury. It is a fundamental necessity for those striving to navigate the complexities of the modern world.

To provide everyone, regardless of background or economic status, with the knowledge and resources necessary to make wise financial decisions, financial empowerment emphasizes the significance of removing obstacles to financial education. This empowerment is a key driver of financial inclusion, promoting economic equality and reducing wealth disparity.

Financial empowerment and knowledge are essential in a world economy that is quickly changing. The ability to navigate financial landscapes, understand investment options, and plan for the future is crucial. Financial empowerment empowers individuals with the knowledge and skills to make sound financial decisions, ensuring long-term security and prosperity.

Moreover, financial empowerment extends beyond personal finance and encompasses the ability to withstand economic challenges and unexpected life events. It involves creating a resilient financial foundation that can weather uncertainties, such as job loss, health emergencies, or economic downturns.

Financial empowerment is also a key driver of social mobility. It transcends individuals, contributing to the overall well-being of communities and societies. People who feel empowered are more likely to make constructive contributions to their communities, which promotes resilience and economic growth on a larger scale.

In essence, financial empowerment is a journey towards financial independence, where individuals are not just recipients of financial advice but active participants in shaping their financial destinies. It is a dynamic and ongoing process that evolves with changing circumstances, helping individuals adapt and thrive in the ever-changing landscape of their financial lives. Ultimately, financial empowerment is a catalyst for personal growth, allowing individuals to achieve their goals, fulfill their aspirations, and attain a sense of overall wellbeing.

1.1 ADVANTAGES OF FINANCIAL EMPOWERMENT

The process of taking charge of one's financial life by obtaining the information, abilities, and tools necessary to make wise financial decisions is known as financial empowerment.

This empowerment brings about numerous advantages that extend beyond individual wellbeing and have a positive impact on communities and societies at large.

Here are some advantages of financial empowerment:

1. **ENHANCED FINANCIAL STABILITY:**
   Financial empowerment enables individuals to build a solid foundation for their economic wellbeing. By cultivating habits such as budgeting, saving, and investing wisely, people can establish a safety net that protects them from unforeseen financial challenges.
2. **INCREASED ECONOMIC MOBILITY:**
   Access to financial education and resources fosters upward economic mobility. Individuals equipped with financial knowledge are better positioned to make strategic career decisions, invest in education, and leverage opportunities for personal and professional growth.

3. **REDUCED STRESS AND ANXIETY:**
   Financial literacy equips individuals with the tools to manage and plan for their financial futures, reducing the stress and anxiety associated with economic uncertainty. This, in turn, has a beneficial effect on one's emotional and mental health.

4. **EMPOWERMENT OF MARGINALIZED COMMUNITIES:**
   Financial empowerment plays a crucial role in addressing economic disparities. Providing marginalized communities with the tools to navigate the financial landscape empowers them to break the cycle of poverty and fosters inclusive economic development.

5. **IMPROVED DECISION-MAKING:**
   Financially empowered individuals are more adept at making informed financial decisions. This extends to choices related to major life events such as homeownership, education, and retirement planning, leading to better long-term outcomes.

6. **STIMULATED ECONOMIC GROWTH:**
   As more individuals gain financial empowerment, there is a ripple effect on the broader economy. Informed consumers contribute to increased economic activity, entrepreneurship, and overall financial health, promoting sustainable economic growth.

7. **ENHANCED RETIREMENT PREPAREDNESS:**
   Financially empowered individuals are more likely to plan for retirement adequately. They understand the importance of saving for the future and taking advantage of investment opportunities, ensuring a more comfortable and secure retirement.

8. **RESILIENCE IN TIMES OF CRISIS:**
   Financially literate individuals are better prepared to navigate economic downturns and unexpected crises. With emergency funds and a solid financial plan in place, they can weather financial storms more effectively.

1.2 POTENTIAL PITFALLS OF FINANCIAL EMPOWERMENT

Jane is over the moon now that she knows more about the many advantages of financial empowerment. However, John is more cautious and warns her about some of the potential pitfalls they must look out for on their journey to financial empowerment.

Financial empowerment, while often touted as a means to improve individual and community well-being, is not without its challenges. It is crucial to recognize the potential pitfalls associated with the pursuit of financial empowerment to ensure a balanced understanding of its implications.

1. **INEQUALITY EXACERBATION:**
   Financial empowerment initiatives may inadvertently widen existing economic disparities. Those who already possess resources and knowledge might benefit more from such programs, leaving marginalized groups further behind. This can reinforce systemic inequalities and create a larger gap between the financially empowered and the economically disenfranchised.

2. **SHORT-TERM FOCUS:**
   Some financial empowerment programs may prioritize short-term gains, such as immediate income generation, over long-term financial stability and education. This narrow focus can lead to challenges in maintaining economic wellbeing over time.

3. **RISK OF EXPLOITATION:**
   In pursuit of financial empowerment, individuals might be exposed to predatory practices or scams. Without proper financial literacy and consumer protection measures, vulnerable individuals may fall victim to fraudulent schemes promising quick financial gains, ultimately exacerbating their economic vulnerabilities.

4. **EMPHASIS ON INDIVIDUALISM:**
   While personal responsibility is a key aspect of financial empowerment, an exclusive focus on individual efforts may undermine the importance of systemic changes. It might

divert attention from addressing structural issues contributing to financial inequality, such as inadequate social safety nets or discriminatory policies.

5. **PSYCHOLOGICAL STRESS:**
Particularly in settings where achieving financial success is linked to one's value as a person, the pressure to succeed financially can exacerbate stress and anxiety. Initiatives aimed at promoting financial empowerment may have the opposite effect on mental health as a result of this stress.

6. **DIGITAL DIVIDE:**
Financial empowerment initiatives may not benefit those with limited access to technology or digital literacy in an increasingly digital financial landscape. Some groups may become even more marginalized as a result of the digital divide, which will make it more difficult for them to take advantage of economic opportunities.

1.3 BUILDING A STRONG FOUNDATION

Achieving long-term financial success and security requires laying a solid financial foundation. Your financial security depends on carefully laid foundations that can endure market swings and unforeseen difficulties, much like a strong building needs a strong foundation.

These are some essential guidelines to help you build and solidify your financial base.

1. **EVALUATE YOUR CURRENT FINANCIAL SITUATION:**
    One of the most important first steps in reaching your long-term financial goals and preserving stability is evaluating your current financial status. Start by looking at your revenue sources, including your pay, bonuses, and any additional sources. Assess whether your income is sufficient to cover your expenses and if there is space for invest-ments or savings.
2. **SAVINGS FOR GOALS:**
    Establish both short- and long-term financial objectives, such as retirement, home owner-ship, and education funding. A specific por-tion of your income should be set aside for saving toward these goals.
3. **BUDGETING:**
    A budget that is made and followed is essen-tial to financial stability. Recognize your earn-ings, keep tabs on your outlays, and set aside money for savings, discretionary spending, and necessities. A carefully thought-out budget guarantees that you live within your

means and have the money set aside for future objectives.

4. **EMERGENCY FUND:**

   An emergency fund is helpful as a financial safety net. Aim for three or six months' worth of living expenses saved in an easily accessible account. This fund can help you avoid using credit cards or loans during difficult times by covering unforeseen medical costs, auto repairs, or temporary unemployment.

5. **DEBT MANAGEMENT:**

   Control and reduce high-interest debt, like credit card debt. You may want to pay off the loans with the highest interest rates first in order of priority. Making a plan to pay off debt can help free up funds for investing and saving, which will improve your long-term financial situation.

6. **INSURANCE COVERAGE:**

   Obtain adequate insurance to protect your assets. This includes property, health, disability, and life insurance. With insurance, you can avoid having unforeseen circumstances impede your ability to achieve your financial goals.

7. **DIVERSIFIED INVESTMENTS:**

   One essential element of accumulating wealth is investing. Investing in a variety of asset classes will help you spread risk and maximize returns. To create an investment plan that fits your time horizon, financial goals, and risk tolerance, speak with a financial advisor.

8. **ESTATE PLANNING:**
   Make sure that your estate is properly planned for so that your assets are safeguarded and distributed in accordance with your wishes. This could entail naming beneficiaries for your accounts, establishing trusts, and drafting a will. Estate planning protects your financial legacy and gives you peace of mind.

9. **TAX EFFICIENCY:**
   Maximize your tax efficiency by taking advantage of available tax credits, deductions, and deferral strategies. Consult with a tax professional to optimize your financial decisions and minimize your tax liability.

10. **FINANCIAL DISCIPLINE:**
    Building a strong financial foundation requires discipline and patience. Avoid impulsive financial decisions and focus on long-term objectives. Consistency in saving, investing, and budgeting will contribute significantly to your financial success over time. Make sure your financial plan stays in line with your objectives by reviewing and adjusting it on a regular basis as circumstances change.

John and Jane learned that financial empowerment involves taking control of finances, fostering security, and making informed decisions. It encompasses literacy, budgeting, and investment, enabling individuals to navigate financial landscapes confidently. It is crucial for economic stability, social mobility, and resilience.

While advantageous, there are pitfalls such as exacerbating inequality and short-term focus. Building a strong foundation involves evaluating finances, saving, budgeting, managing debt, investing diversely, planning estates, having insurance, and maintaining financial discipline.

2

EVALUATING YOUR PRESENT FINANCIAL CONDITION

After some discussions, Jane is worried that John does not have an accurate reading of their financial condition. She knows gaining a proper view is the first order of business but how do they go about doing that?

To properly evaluate your current financial situation, start by looking at your revenue sources, including your pay, bonuses, and any additional sources. Assess whether your income is sufficient to cover your expenses and if there is space for investments or savings.

Next, scrutinize your monthly expenditures. Categorize your spending into essential and non-essential categories. Essential expenses include housing, utilities, groceries, and insurance, while non-essential items may encompass entertainment, dining out, and luxury purchases. Ensure that your essential expenses are well within your means, leaving room for discretionary spending or saving.

Review your debt obligations, such as credit cards, loans, or mortgages. Calculate the total outstanding balance and interest. Create a plan to systematically manage and pay off your debt, giving priority to loans with high interest rates.

Analyze your emergency fund and savings. A strong financial strategy has a safety net to pay for unforeseen costs. If you have too little in your emergency fund, consider reallocating some money to make up for it.

Evaluate your investments and retirement accounts. Assess the performance of your portfolio, diversification, and whether it aligns with your risk tolerance and long-term objectives. Adjust your investment strategy, if necessary, to optimize returns.

Finally, consider your financial goals, both short-term and long-term. Whether it is saving for a home, education, or retirement, ensure your current financial situation aligns with these objectives. Adjust your budget and savings plan accordingly.

Regularly revisiting and reassessing your financial situation is essential as circumstances change. You can overcome financial obstacles and work toward a safe and prosperous future by remaining proactive and making wise decisions.

Let's take a closer look at some of the steps to take when assessing your financial situation.

2.1 CREATE A PERSONAL FINANCIAL SNAPSHOT

A personal financial snapshot is a crucial tool for gaining a clear understanding of your current financial situation and planning for your future. This snapshot provides a comprehensive overview of your income, expenses, assets, and liabilities. By compiling this information, you can make informed decisions about budgeting, saving, investing, and achieving your financial goals. Here's a guide on how to create your financial snapshot.

1. **GATHER INCOME INFORMATION:**
   The first pillar of the analysis is *income*, encompassing all sources of earnings or money coming in. This includes salaries, bonuses, freelance income, investments, and any additional revenue streams. Make sure you have a clear and accurate understanding of your entire income and note the after-tax

amounts to reflect your actual take-home pay. Regular and irregular income sources should be clearly distinguished to facilitate a refined analysis.

2. **DETAIL YOUR EXPENSES:**

   On the flip side, *expenses* represent the financial outflows or money going out, covering everything from daily expenditures to recurring bills and debt repayments. Categorize and list all your monthly expenses. This should cover both *fixed costs* like rent or mortgage, utilities, insurance, and *variable costs* such as groceries, dining out, entertainment, and transportation. Be thorough in capturing all aspects of your spending habits. A meticulous examination of each expense category aids in understanding where money is going and whether it aligns with your financial goals.

3. **CALCULATE NET CASH FLOW:**

   Net cash flow is the difference between the cash coming in and the cash going out. To find your *net cash flow*, deduct all of your total expenses from all of your income. A positive figure denotes a surplus, whereas a negative figure denotes a deficit. Understanding your cash flow is essential for proficient budgetary planning and pinpointing opportunities for cost reduction.

4. **LIST ASSETS:**

   Assets are things you *own* that have value. Identify and document all your assets, including savings accounts, investments, real estate, and valuable possessions. Assign each asset a monetary value. This step provides insight into your overall wealth and helps in assessing your financial health.

5. **DETERMINE LIABILITIES:**
   Liabilities are things you *owe*. Enumerate all of your debts, including credit card debt, mortgages, auto loans, and school loans. Planning to reduce your debt and assessing your debt-to-income ratio requires an understanding of your liabilities.

6. **CALCULATE NET WORTH:**
   Your net worth is one of the most significant indicators of your financial health and a helpful tool for long-term financial planning. To put it simply, your net worth is the amount of money you would still have after paying off all of your debts. Subtract all of your liabilities from all of your assets to determine your net worth. Understanding your net worth allows you to assess your current position on the path to financial empowerment.

7. **REVIEW INSURANCE COVERAGE:**
   Insurance coverage should be examined when assessing your financial situation. Do your life, health, property, and any other pertinent insurance provide adequate coverage? To safeguard your assets and reduce financial risk, you must evaluate your insurance coverage.

8. **EVALUATE SAVINGS:**
   The analysis should shed light on the allocation of funds towards savings and investments. *Savings* act as a financial safety net, providing a buffer for unexpected expenses, while *investments* offer opportunities for wealth accumulation over time. Have you set aside a certain amount of money each month for investments and savings? Long-term savings, such as retirement savings and investments, are necessary to build wealth. Evaluating the percentage of income devoted to savings and investments provides valuable insights into one's commitment to long-term financial goals.

9. **SET FINANCIAL GOALS:**
   Given your existing circumstances, set both short- and long-term financial goals. Setting clear financial objectives will guide your decisions, whether you're investing for retirement, paying off debt, or saving for a down payment.

10. **UPDATE YOUR SNAPSHOT REGULARLY:**
    Financial situations can change, so it is important to update your financial snapshot regularly. Review and adjust your plan as needed, especially after major life events such as marriage, the birth of a child, or a career change.

Creating a personal financial snapshot is an ongoing process that empowers you to take control of your financial future. By regularly revisiting and refining this snapshot, you can make informed decisions, build wealth, and achieve your financial goals.

As John and Jane set out on their financial adventure, they first evaluate their current situation by reviewing their debt, spending, and income. They assess their assets, liabilities, and insurance coverage to get a thorough financial picture.

Throughout their journey, they will stay proactive in managing life's changes and attaining financial stability and prosperity by updating their strategy on a regular basis.

John and Jane are excited, and truthfully, a bit nervous as they are now on their way to financial empowerment.

3

SETTING FINANCIAL GOALS

John and Jane set a time to look at their financial goals together. John is excited and decides to get a head start by listing the goals he believes they should share as a family. Does John have the right idea about setting financial goals?

Setting specific, attainable financial goals offers a path forward for your financial journey, regardless of your stage in life—you may be embarking on a new career, saving for a significant event, or seeking long-term financial stability.

Having finished evaluating your existing financial status, you can now start establishing your financial objectives. Making realistic goals that fit your circumstances will be easier if you are aware of your current financial condition.

Strike a balance between present needs and long-term ambitions by setting short-, medium-, and long-term objectives. While long-term goals require strategic planning and disciplined saving, short-term goals offer immediate rewards and increase motivation.

Short-term objectives may include:

- Creating an emergency fund.
- Paying off high-interest debt.
- Saving money for a trip.

Medium-term goals may include:

- Starting a business.
- Funding a child's education.
- Saving money for a down payment on a house.

Long-term planning may include things such as:

- Leaving a legacy.
- Accumulating wealth.
- Creating retirement plans.

Think about your goals' order of importance. Certain objectives might be more crucial or urgent than others. Consider paying off high-interest debt first because the interest can mount quickly and impede your ability to make progress with your finances. After taking care of your immediate issues, concentrate on achieving your long-term financial objectives.

Evaluate and adjust your financial plan as circumstances warrant. Review and modify your financial goals on a regular basis in response to changing circumstances. Life is dynamic, so, as priorities, income levels, and economic conditions change, so should your financial goals. By regularly evaluating your financial plan, you can stay on course and make necessary adjustments. To help you reach your objectives, make use of available tools and resources.

For assistance creating a thorough financial plan suited to your goals, consider consulting with a financial advisor. To keep track of your progress and make wise financial decisions, use retirement calculators, investing tools, and budgeting apps.

3.1 SMART GOAL SETTING

John provides a list of financial goals, but Jane says they need SMART goals. John is insulted. Is Jane calling him dumb? No, in fact, SMART is an acronym...

Setting goals is an essential part of both personal and professional growth. However, not all goals are created equal. Establish objectives to improve your chances of success. Objectives ought to be *S*pecific, *M*easurable, *A*chievable, *R*elevant, and *T*ime-bound (*SMART*). This method provides goal-setting with a well-defined structure that improves accountability, motivation, and attention.

3.1.1 SPECIFIC FINANCIAL GOALS

Objectives ought to be precise and well-defined. A goal is easier to understand and work toward the more specific it is. Ambiguous objectives may need to be clarified. For example, rather than "exercise more," a specific goal might be to "run for 30 minutes every morning."

EXAMPLES OF SPECIFIC FINANCIAL GOALS

SAVING FOR A DOWN PAYMENT ON A HOME:

- Specific Goal: Save $50,000 within the next five years for a down payment on a house.
- This goal is specific in terms of the amount ($50,000), the purpose (down payment), and the timeframe (five years).

RETIREMENT SAVINGS:

- Specific Goal: Contribute $500 per month to a retirement savings account for the next 30 years.
- This goal is specific in terms of the monthly contribution amount ($500), the goal (retirement savings), and the duration (30 years).

EMERGENCY FUND BUILDING:

- Specific Goal: Accumulate three months' worth of living expenses, totaling $15,000, in an emergency fund within the next 12 months.
- This goal is specific in terms of the amount ($15,000), the purpose (emergency fund), and the timeframe (12 months).

3.1.2 MEASURABLE FINANCIAL GOALS

Measuring progress is vital for staying motivated and on track. Goals should include concrete criteria to assess progress objectively. If the goal is to "improve sales," a measurable goal would be to "increase monthly sales by 15%."

EXAMPLES OF MEASURABLE FINANCIAL GOALS

SAVE $10,000 FOR AN EMERGENCY FUND:

This goal is measurable because it specifies a target amount of $10,000.

You can track your progress by regularly checking your savings account balance.

Once you reach the $10,000 mark, you will know you've achieved your goal.

REDUCE MONTHLY EXPENSES BY 15%:

- This goal is measurable as it includes a specific percentage, 15%.
- You can track your monthly spending and compare it to the initial baseline.
- Achieving a consistent 15% reduction will indicate success.

INCREASE ANNUAL INCOME TO $75,000:

- This goal is measurable, with a clear target income of $75,000 per year.
- You can track your income through pay stubs, tax documents, or financial statements.
- Once your income reaches or exceeds $75,000, you've achieved this financial goal.

3.1.3 ACHIEVABLE FINANCIAL GOALS

As important as it is to aim high, objectives should also be reachable and practical. Goals that are not realistic or achievable can cause demotivation and dissatisfaction. Evaluate your present skills and resources. If you're an amateur runner, it could be challenging to set a goal to complete a marathon next month. A more achievable goal might be to finish a 5K in three months.

EXAMPLES OF ACHIEVABLE FINANCIAL GOALS

ESTABLISH AN EMERGENCY FUND:

- Goal: Save three to six months' worth of living expenses in an easily accessible account.
- Rationale: In the event of unforeseen costs, such as auto repairs, medical issues, or job loss, an emergency fund offers stability and safety.

DEBT REPAYMENT:

- Goal: Pay off high-interest debt (e.g., credit card debt) within a specific timeframe.
- Rationale: Reducing and eliminating high-interest debt can free up money for

other financial goals, improve credit scores, and reduce financial stress.

RETIREMENT SAVINGS:

- Goal: Contribute a certain percentage of income to a retirement savings account.
- Rationale: Building a substantial retirement fund is crucial for financial security in later years. Consistent contributions over time, especially when starting early, can take advantage of compound interest.

3.1.4 RELEVANT FINANCIAL GOALS

Your goals should be pertinent to your values and aspirations and should line up with your overall objectives. Make sure every objective advances your main objective. "Complete an online coding course" is a relevant goal if your long-term goal is to work as a software developer, as opposed to unrelated ones like "learn to play the guitar."

EXAMPLES OF RELEVANT FINANCIAL GOALS

EMERGENCY FUND:

To maintain financial stability, you should keep three to six months' worth of living expenditures in a readily accessible account. This fund may be extremely help-ful in the event of unanticipated events such as medical emergencies, job loss or unexpected expenses.

RETIREMENT SAVINGS:

Planning for retirement is a significant financial goal. Setting aside a portion of income in retirement accounts can ensure a comfortable and secure retirement. The goal may involve estimating future expenses, factoring in inflation, and making regular contributions to retirement accounts.

DEBT REPAYMENT:

Managing and eventually eliminating high-interest debt is another important financial goal. This might include paying off credit card balances, student loans, or other debts. Making a plan to pay off debt will help you achieve financial stability and free up funds for other objectives like investing or saving.

3.1.5 TIME-BOUND FINANCIAL GOALS

Establishing deadlines helps people feel urgency and avoids procrastination. Goals might not be completed if they have no deadline. An example of a time-bound goal would be, "finish the first draft of the book within six months," as opposed to just saying, "write a book."

EXAMPLES OF TIME-BOUND FINANCIAL GOALS

EMERGENCY FUND ACCUMULATION (SHORT-TERM):

- Goal: Save $5,000 in an emergency fund.
- Time Frame: Achieve this goal within the next 12 months.
- Rationale: A short-term goal like this guarantees easy access to money in case of unforeseen costs and offers financial security.

DOWN PAYMENT FOR A HOME (MEDIUM-TERM):

- Goal: Save $30,000 for a down payment on a house.
- Time Frame: Achieve this goal within the next five years.
- Rationale: Planning to buy a home is a medium-term goal, and setting a specific time frame helps in saving toward a significant financial milestone.

RETIREMENT SAVINGS (LONG-TERM):

- Goal: Accumulate $1 million in retirement savings.
- Time Frame: Achieve this goal in the next 25 years.

- Rationale: Saving for retirement is a long-term financial goal. The specific time frame allows for strategic investment planning and compounding to build a substantial retirement fund.

3.2 PRIORITIZING GOALS BASED ON URGENCY AND IMPACT

An essential component of efficient time and resource management is setting goals in order of importance and urgency. The secret to success in any undertaking, whether personal or professional, is the ability to recognize and concentrate on things that require immediate attention while taking their possible repercussions into account. This process ensures that efforts are concentrated where they matter most, optimizing productivity and achieving meaningful results.

Urgency refers to the time-sensitivity of a task—how quickly it needs to be addressed or completed. Impact, on the other hand, refers to the significance of a task's outcome and its potential to influence the overall objective. A successful prioritization strategy involves finding the delicate balance between these two factors.

First and foremost, tasks with both high urgency and high impact should be given top priority. These are the critical issues that demand immediate attention and, when addressed, can lead to substantial positive outcomes. For instance, meeting a pressing deadline for a major project or resolving a critical issue that could otherwise impede progress falls into this category. By addressing these tasks first, you ensure that your efforts have the maximum potential for positive influence.

Next in line are tasks with high impact but lower urgency. While these tasks might demand little attention, they contribute significantly to the long-term goals and success of a project or objective. Investing time in strategic planning, skill development, or building relationships can fall into this category. Though not urgent, neglecting these tasks may hinder future progress, so allocating time and resources to them is essential for sustained success.

Conversely, tasks with high urgency but lower impact should be approached cautiously. While they demand immediate attention, their long-term influence on the overall goal may be limited. Handling these tasks efficiently is necessary, but it is crucial to keep them from overshadowing more impactful priorities. Delegating or streamlining processes can be effective in managing such tasks without compromising the focus on high-impact activities.

Tasks with both low urgency and low impact may be considered lower priority. These tasks contribute minimally to immediate goals and can be deferred or addressed with less urgency. While they should be addressed, allocating excessive time and resources to these tasks may divert attention from more critical matters.

Adopting a systematic approach, such as the Eisenhower Matrix, can facilitate the prioritization process. This matrix categorizes tasks into four quadrants based on urgency and importance, guiding individuals to focus on tasks that are both urgent and important and then gradually moving down the priority list.

John is now well aware of what it means to attain SMART (Specific, Measurable, Achievable, Relevant, and Time-bound) goals. He and Jane set and prioritize their goals based on urgency and impact to optimize productivity and achieve meaningful results. They define each goal as either short term, medium term, or long term. They could see that understanding their current situation first, helped them better define their goals. They research and use tools like the Eisenhower Matrix to help them focus their efforts where they matter most.

To further enhance their plan, John contacts Fred, a financial adviser who is highly recommended by a colleague. Although it is a lot of work and takes them some time to complete, they understand that this is an important step in their journey to financial empowerment.

4

ESTABLISHING A REASONABLE BUDGET

John has his eye on a new grill, but Jane warns that they should do their budget before adding any further expenses.

Now that you have a starting point in your journey to financial empowerment and have identified your goals, you are ready to establish a budget. Whether you are in charge of managing your finances or the budget for a business, your financial journey is guided by a well-planned budget.

Budgeting is a crucial financial instrument that helps people and companies alike manage their finances effectively. Many of the items discussed in the previous section while creating your financial snapshot will be revisited in establishing your budget. A budget is a detailed plan with goals for income, savings, and expenses over a specified period. Comprehending the principles of budgeting is imperative in attaining individual financial stability.

Create a monthly budget by compiling all of your financial data. A certain percentage of your income should be set aside for each category of expenses. Be fair and consider unanticipated costs. Strive for equilibrium to enable you to fulfill your monetary commitments and sustain a pleasant lifestyle. Be realistic.

Use these essential steps to create a realistic budget:

1. **UNDERSTAND YOUR INCOME:**
   The income listed in your initial financial snapshot could be the starting point for your budget. Know your sources of income and their frequency. Create a comprehensive list to ensure that you're accounting for all financial inflows. Begin by assessing your sources of income from your snapshot. This includes your salary, freelance gigs, side hustles, or any other monetary inflow. Make sure you have a clear and accurate understanding of your income.

2. **LIST YOUR EXPENSES:**
   The expenses listed in your initial financial snapshot could be the starting point for your

budget. Make a thorough record of every expense you incur. Sort them into two categories: fixed and variable costs. Rent or a mortgage, utilities, insurance, and loan payments are examples of fixed expenses. Groceries, entertainment, eating out, and other discretionary expenditures are all considered variable expenses. Categorize your expenses to gain insight into spending patterns and identify areas for potential savings.

3. **DISTINGUISH NEEDS FROM WANTS:**
   Differentiate between essential needs and non-essential wants. While some expenses, like housing and food, are necessities, others, such as dining out or subscription services, fall into the discretionary category. Prioritize your needs and allocate funds accordingly.

4. **SET REALISTIC GOALS**:
   Establish short-term and long-term financial goals. Whether it is saving for a vacation, building an emergency fund, or paying off debt, having clear objectives helps you allocate resources effectively. Ensure that your goals are SMART—specific, measurable, achievable, relevant, and time-bound.

5. **EMERGENCY FUND:**
   An often-overlooked aspect of a budget is establishing and maintaining an emergency fund. This emergency fund is intended to cover unanticipated costs, like unexpected medical bills or a sudden loss of employment.

This safety net can help you avoid using credit cards or loans when things get hard.

6. **DEBT REPAYMENT PLAN:**

Make a repayment plan if you have any outstanding debts. You may want to consider paying off high-interest debts first to reduce interest over time, but this is just one option for debt repayment. We will look at other options later in this book. While still fulfilling your other financial commitments, set aside a specific amount of your budget for debt repayment.

7. **SAVINGS AND INVESTMENTS:**

Make sure that your budget includes a non-negotiable category for savings. Set aside a certain amount of money each month for investments and savings. No matter the amount, regular contributions are essential whether you're setting aside money for a particular purpose or creating a general savings account. Look into investing options that fit your financial goals and risk tolerance to diversify your financial holdings. Long-term savings and investment are necessary for building wealth. To maintain consistency, consider automating contributions to your investment and savings accounts.

8. **LEVERAGE BUDGETING TOOLS AND APPS TO STREAMLINE THE PROCESS:**

Numerous tools can classify your spending, automatically track your expenses, and reveal information about your financial habits. Making use of technology can make budgeting more efficient and manageable.

9. **SEEK PROFESSIONAL ADVICE:**
   Financial planners, advisers, or accountants can offer insightful advice and help you optimize your budget. A specialist can offer tailored advice based on your particular financial circumstances and objectives. They can provide you with tactics, advice, and insights to help you make wise financial choices.

10. **REVIEW AND ADJUST:**
    Your budget should be reviewed and adjusted frequently. Because life is dynamic, things change. Be adaptable and make changes as necessary. If you discover that you frequently go over budget in a certain area, you might want to think about reallocating money or finding other ways to save on expenses. Regular reviews also help you recognize areas for improvement and celebrate your financial successes.

John is anxious and wants to get a head-start on the budget. He calculates their monthly income from all sources, including Jane's side hustles. He prioritizes their regular expenses such as mortgage and utilities like gas, water, phone, and electricity. He also allocates funds for non-regular expenses such as dining out, entertainment, and debt repayment.

And, of course, John remembers to include the grill he has been eyeing in the budget under the 'Other' category.

A vacation overseas to visit Jane's family is coming up this year, so he includes a regular amount to save for the vacation in their budget.

John is ready to review the budget with Jane. Did he include everything to ensure a thorough and complete budget?

5

MAINTAINING AN EMERGENCY FUND

Using his math wizardry, John has mapped out the most efficient way to allocate all the family funds. However, Jane advises him that his "efficiency" neglects putting money away. Rather than spending everything on hand, she has some ideas about saving up in case of an emergency...

Establishing and maintaining an emergency fund is essential to financial planning because it serves as a safety net in the event of unanticipated expenses or financial hardships. This fund should be included in your budget and serves as a cushion against unforeseen circumstances, offering peace of mind and stability in times of need. By implementing the methods and strategies outlined in this section, you can build and maintain a robust emergency fund, providing financial resilience and peace of mind in the face of unexpected challenges. Keep in mind that successfully maintaining an emergency fund requires a combination of consistency, discipline, and flexibility.

It would be best if you did not underestimate the significance of emergency savings, and the following are the main justifications for why creating and keeping such a fund is crucial:

1. **FINANCIAL SECURITY:**
   Emergency savings serve as a kind of financial safety net, protecting you and your family from unforeseen costs like home maintenance, auto repairs, or medical emergencies. You can better manage these unforeseen expenses without turning to credit cards or high-interest loans if you have a safety net in place.
2. **JOB LOSS OR INCOME REDUCTION:**
   Economic uncertainties, industry changes, or unexpected job loss can significantly impact income. Emergency savings provide a buffer during periods of unemployment or reduced income, helping cover essential living expenses until a new job is secured.
3. **HEALTHCARE EXPENSES:**
   Medical emergencies can arise at any time, leading to unexpected healthcare expenses if

they are not covered through a government or employment plan. When it comes to making sure that you and your family can get essential medical care without jeopardizing your financial stability, emergency reserves can be a lifesaver.

4. **PEACE OF MIND:**
   It is reassuring to know that a financial safety net is in place. You may be less stressed and anxious about unforeseen financial burdens when you have this sense of security, which enables you to face life's obstacles with more confidence.

5. **AVOIDING DEBT ACCUMULATION:**
   Individuals with emergency savings are better equipped to deal with unanticipated costs without taking out loans or credit card debt. This may eventually result in debt accumulation and financial strain. With savings, you can break free from the debt cycle.

6. **OPPORTUNITY TO SEIZE OPPORTUNITIES:**
   Emergency savings not only protect against unexpected hardships but also provide the flexibility to seize opportunities. Whether pursuing further education, changing careers, or investing in a business venture, having savings can empower individuals to take calculated risks.

7. **NATURAL DISASTERS AND HOME REPAIRS:**
   Property damage can be greatly increased by natural disasters such as floods and earth-

quakes. Emergency savings are crucial following such events to cover any required repairs or transient moving expenses.

8. **FAMILY SUPPORT:**
Emergency savings extend beyond personal benefits and can also support family members in times of need. Whether assisting aging parents, helping siblings facing financial challenges, or supporting children through unexpected situations, having savings allows for a more robust support system.

9. **RETIREMENT PLANNING:**
Emergency savings complement long-term financial planning, such as retirement savings. Having a separate fund for emergencies ensures that retirement savings remain untouched and can continue to grow undisturbed.

10. **FLEXIBILITY IN BUDGETING:**
Emergency savings provide flexibility in budgeting by allowing individuals to allocate funds for unexpected expenses without disrupting their regular budget. This flexibility enhances overall financial stability.

5.1 BUILDING AND MAINTAINING AN EMERGENCY FUND

Here are some essentials to consider when building and maintaining an emergency fund:

1. **SET REALISTIC GOALS:**
   Begin by assessing your monthly expenses and determining an appropriate target for your emergency fund. Some financial advisors advise setting aside three to six months' worth of living expenses.

2. **PRIORITIZE LIQUIDITY:**
   Opt for liquid and easily accessible assets when building your emergency fund. Generally, a money market account or savings account would be a good option because they provide a small return along with liquidity. Avoid investments with higher risk and lower liquidity, as the primary goal of an emergency fund is quick access to funds when needed.

3. **CONSISTENT CONTRIBUTIONS:**
   Building an emergency fund requires discipline and consistency. Establish a monthly savings goal and treat it as a non-negotiable expense. Automating transfers to your emergency fund ensures that you contribute consistently, even when faced with other financial obligations.

4. **REASSESS AND ADJUST:**
   Review your financial status on a regular basis and evaluate how sufficient your emergency fund is. Your savings objectives should adapt to your changing circumstances. Adjust your targets and contributions as needed, ensuring that your emergency fund remains aligned with your current financial landscape.

5. **MITIGATE INSURANCE GAPS:**
   While an emergency fund is crucial, it is not a substitute for insurance. Evaluate your insurance coverage for health, property, and income protection. Adequate insurance can complement your emergency fund by covering certain unexpected costs, reducing the financial burden on your savings.

6. **DEFERRED LONG-TERM INVESTMENTS:**
   This term emphasizes the delay or postponement of investments aimed at long-term growth, as resources are redirected towards building and maintaining an emergency fund. It highlights how the allocation of financial resources in the short term may defer opportunities for long-term wealth accumulation.

7. **OPPORTUNITY COST OF EMERGENCY PREPAREDNESS:**
   This concept underscores the idea that prioritizing emergency preparedness comes with an opportunity cost—the potential benefits foregone by not allocating those resources to long-term goals. It reflects the trade-off

between immediate financial security and the potential gains or achievements associated with pursuing long-term objectives.

8. **IMPACT ON LONG-TERM GOALS:**
   Channeling significant funds into an emergency fund might slow down progress toward long-term financial goals, such as retirement savings or major investments. Striking the right balance is essential.

9. **VARYING DEFINITIONS OF EMERGENCIES:**
   Individuals may have different definitions of what constitutes an emergency. Some might dip into the fund for non-urgent expenses, potentially undermining the fund's purpose.

10. **FINANCIAL EDUCATION AND PLANNING:**
    Educate yourself on financial planning and literacy to make informed decisions about your emergency fund. Financial resilience can be improved by employing efficient budgeting techniques and distinguishing between essential and non-essential expenses.

11. **STAY RESILIENT DURING FINANCIAL CHALLENGES:**
    In times of financial stress, it is essential to stay focused on your long-term goals. Avoid impulsive decisions that could deplete your emergency fund unnecessarily. Lean on your financial plan and consider seeking professional advice if faced with complex challenges.

5.2 STRATEGIES FOR CREATING AND KEEPING AN EMERGENCY FUND

To establish and sustain an emergency fund effectively, consider the following strategies:

1. **SET CLEAR GOALS:**
   Define the purpose of your emergency fund. Whether it is covering three to six months' worth of living expenses, medical emergencies, or unexpected home or car repairs, having a specific goal will guide your savings efforts.
2. **ESTABLISH A REALISTIC BUDGET:**
   Examine your monthly earnings and outgoings to ascertain the amount you can reasonably contribute to your emergency reserve. Make a budget that covers regular contributions without sacrificing necessities for subsistence.
3. **START SMALL, BUT START TODAY:**
   Don't be discouraged if you can't immediately save a large sum. Begin with a modest amount that won't strain your budget. Consistency is key, and over time, you can increase your contributions as your financial situation improves.
4. **AUTOMATE SAVINGS:**
   Establish recurring transfers from your main account to an emergency fund account.

Automation reduces the temptation to spend money elsewhere and enables you to automatically set aside a portion of your income for an emergency fund.

5. **PRIORITIZE HIGH-INTEREST DEBT:**
   While building an emergency fund is important, it is equally crucial to address high-interest debt. To eventually have more money for savings, you may want to consider paying off high-interest debt first.

6. **USE WINDFALLS AND BONUSES:**
   Allocate unexpected windfalls, such as tax refunds, work bonuses, or monetary gifts, to your emergency fund. These additional funds can significantly boost your savings without affecting your regular budget.

7. **CUT UNNECESSARY EXPENSES:**
   Determine areas where you can save money by analyzing your spending habits. Put any savings from cutting non-essential spending back into your emergency fund. Over time, little daily expenditure adjustments can add up to significant savings.

8. **REASSESS AND ADJUST:**
   Review your budget and emergency fund goals periodically. As your financial situation evolves, adjust your contributions and goals accordingly. Regular reassessment ensures that your emergency fund remains aligned with your current needs.

9. **SEPARATE THE EMERGENCY FUND FROM DAILY ACCOUNTS:**
   Create a different savings account that is only used for your emergency fund. This separation reduces the likelihood of tapping into the fund for non-emergencies and reinforces the idea that these funds are reserved for unforeseen circumstances.

10. **RESIST TEMPTATION:**
    Stay disciplined and avoid using your emergency fund for non-emergencies. A well-defined emergency fund serves as a financial safety net, and dipping into it for non-essential expenses weakens its effectiveness.

11. **EDUCATE AND INVOLVE FAMILY MEMBERS:**
    Ensure that all family members understand the purpose of the emergency fund and contribute to its success. Involving the entire family creates a sense of shared responsibility and commitment to financial security.

12. **REVIEW AND CELEBRATE MILESTONES:**
    Celebrate each milestone reached in your emergency fund journey. Recognizing your progress can motivate you to stay on track and reinforce positive financial habits.

John realizes that establishing and maintaining an emergency fund is vital for financial stability, offering a safety net against unexpected expenses and hardships. It ensures security, prevents debt accumulation, and provides flexibility.

Strategies include setting goals, consistent contributions, and prioritizing liquidity. It is essential to resist temptation and reassess regularly to align with changing circumstances. John and Jane review their budget together and adjust it to include an emergency fund.

6

STRATEGIES FOR MANAGING DEBT

John and Jane still have those high credit card debts to deal with. How do they do it? John wants to pay off smaller debts a little at a time, but Jane prefers to focus on paying off high interest rate debt first. Let's explore some options and strategies for effective debt management and elimination.

Debt can be a double-edged sword, serving as a means to achieve certain goals but also posing a financial burden. It is important to understand your outstanding debts, their interest rates, and their impact on your overall financial health. Developing a strategy for debt repayment is crucial to alleviating financial stress and paving the way for future financial growth.

6.1 IDENTIFYING DEBT AND ITS IMPACT

Debt, a ubiquitous financial concept, plays a pivotal role in shaping individuals' economic landscape. It can be a powerful tool for growth and investment, but when mishandled, it has the potential to spiral into a cycle of financial instability. It is critical to identify debt and understand its consequences in order to maintain a healthy financial position and make prudent financial decisions.

Debt comes in various forms, ranging from personal loans and credit cards to corporate bonds and government borrowings. At its core, debt represents borrowed money that must be repaid with interest over a specified period. The key is to distinguish between 'good' and 'bad' debt. Good debt is often associated with investments that have the potential to generate future income or enhance one's financial standing. Examples include student loans, mortgages for a home, or loans for starting a business. These debts, when managed responsibly, can contribute to long-term financial wellbeing.

Conversely, bad debt arises from frivolous spending or financing depreciating assets. Credit card debt, often accompanied by high-interest rates, is a classic example. Accumulation of bad debt can lead to a precarious financial situation where the burden of repayment outpaces income growth. Identifying the types of debt you carry is a great step toward responsible financial management.

The impact of debt is multifaceted, influencing individuals, businesses, and the overall economy. Individuals who have too much debt may experience stress, strained relationships, and a lower standard of living. It reduces financial freedom by limiting possibilities for unforeseen costs or future investments. Furthermore, a high debt load can have a negative impact on credit scores and increase the difficulty of obtaining favorable terms on new loans.

To mitigate the negative impacts of debt, you must adopt prudent financial practices. If you are looking for financial security, budgeting, saving, and staying out of debt are essential.

6.2 STRATEGIES FOR EFFECTIVE DEBT MANAGEMENT AND ELIMINATION

Achieving financial stability and independence in today's ever-changing economic environment requires managing and getting rid of debt effectively. Developing a thorough debt management strategy is crucial, regardless of the type of debt you're dealing with, whether it is student loans, credit card debt, or other debt. Here are important methods for efficiently managing and getting rid of debt to give you a road map to take control of your financial situation.

1. **CREATE A DETAILED BUDGET:**
   The foundation of successful debt management is a well-crafted budget. List all of your sources of income and group your monthly expenses first. This clear overview will help identify areas where spending can be trimmed, creating surplus funds that can be directed toward debt repayment.

2. **PRIORITIZE HIGH-INTEREST DEBTS:**
   Not every debt is created equal. Establish a priority list for the debts with the highest interest rates (such as credit card debt). Adding more funds to these high-interest loans lowers the interest accumulated and expedites the repayment of the entire debt.

3. **EMERGENCY FUND:**
   Creating an emergency fund serves as a safety net for your finances, keeping you from having to use credit in unanticipated circumstances. To protect yourself from unforeseen circumstances and avoid taking on additional debt, aim for an emergency fund that is three to six months' worth of living expenses.

4. **NEGOTIATE LOWER INTEREST RATES:**
   Contact your creditors to negotiate lower interest rates. Many lenders are willing to work with borrowers who demonstrate a commitment to repaying their debts. Over

time, a lower interest rate can result in a much smaller total amount repaid.

5. **DEBT CONSOLIDATION:**
   Explore the option of consolidating multiple debts into a single, more manageable loan. This can simplify monthly payments and, if secured at a lower interest rate, reduce over-all interest costs. However, exercise caution and research terms and fees associated with debt consolidation thoroughly.

6. **SNOWBALL VS. AVALANCHE METHOD:**
   There are two common ways to pay off debt: the avalanche and snowball methods. Paying off the smallest debts first gives the snowball method momentum as each debt is paid off. To reduce total interest expenses, the ava-lanche technique gives priority to debts with high interest rates. Decide which strategy best meets your financial goals and preferences.

7. **SEEK PROFESSIONAL GUIDANCE:**
   If managing debt becomes overwhelming, consider seeking advice from financial pro-fessionals. Credit counseling organizations can offer invaluable assistance when it comes to budgeting, negotiating with creditors, and creating a personalized debt management plan.

8. **STAY DISCIPLINED AND CONSISTENT:**
   Consistency is key to debt elimination. Stick to your budget, make timely payments, and resist the temptation to incur additional debt.

Recognize little accomplishments along the road to strengthen sound financial practices.

9. **FINANCIAL LITERACY:**
   Invest time in enhancing your financial literacy. Understanding the principles of personal finance empowers you to make informed decisions, avoid common pitfalls, and navigate the path to debt freedom more effectively.

10. **CELEBRATE PROGRESS:**
    Celebrate your progress and accomplishments as you pay off debt. Acknowledging successes, no matter how minor, can keep one motivated and dedicated to the ultimate objective of debt freedom.

6.3 DEVELOPING A DEBT REPAYMENT PLAN

While managing debt can be difficult, having a well-thought-out plan for paying off debt can offer momentum toward financial independence. Whether you are managing student loans, credit card debt, or other financial obligations, it is critical to take a strategic approach. This is a step-by-step guide to assist you in creating a successful debt repayment strategy.

1. **ASSESS YOUR DEBT:**
   Begin by compiling details regarding every debt you have. Make a detailed list of all your

debts, including the creditor, amount owed, interest rate, and required minimum payment each month. You will be able to see your financial situation clearly with this snapshot.

2. **PRIORITIZE YOUR DEBTS:**
Not all debts are equal. Set a debt hierarchy according to interest rates. The priority should go to paying off high-interest debts like credit card debt, which can mount quickly and impede your ability to make other financial progress.

3. **SET REALISTIC GOALS:**
Set reasonable and attainable objectives for paying off your debt. Divide your objectives into smaller, more doable benchmarks. This will motivate you as you advance, little by little.

4. **CREATE A BUDGET:**
Develop a detailed budget that outlines your monthly income and expenses. Identify areas where you can cut costs and allocate more funds toward debt repayment. Make wise financial decisions by using a well-defined budget.

5. **EMERGENCY FUND:**
While focusing on debt repayment, it is essential to have a small emergency fund. This fund can cover unexpected expenses, preventing you from relying on credit cards and derailing your debt repayment progress.

6. **NEGOTIATE INTEREST RATES:**
   Make an effort to bargain for reduced interest rates with your creditors. Reduced interest rates expedite the debt repayment process by allocating a larger portion of your payment toward the principal.

7. **CONSIDER DEBT CONSOLIDATION:**
   Explore consolidating high-interest debts into a single, lower-interest loan. This can simplify your repayment process and save you money on interest.

8. **SNOWBALL VS. AVALANCHE METHOD:**
   Select a debt repayment plan that makes sense for your spending habits and financial circumstances. Using the snowball method, you start by paying off the smallest debt and build momentum as you pay them off one by one. By focusing on high-interest debts initially, the avalanche technique reduces total interest payments.

9. **MONITOR YOUR PROGRESS:**
   Review your debt repayment plan regularly and adjust it as needed. Celebrate milestones along the way to keep yourself motivated. If unexpected expenses arise, modify your plan accordingly to maintain sight of your ultimate goal.

10. **SEEK PROFESSIONAL ADVICE:**
    If your debt is complicated or overwhelming, seek advice from a credit counseling service or financial advisor. They can offer you indi-

vidualized advice and help you deal with difficult financial situations.

6.4 AVALANCHE VS. SNOWBALL TECHNIQUE

There are two common ways to pay off debt, especially multiple debts with different interest rates: the *Snowball* and the *Avalanche* methods. While the goal of both approaches is to pay off debt efficiently, their approaches and priorities are different.

1. **SNOWBALL METHOD:**

Regardless of interest rates, the goal of the Snowball method of debt repayment is to pay off the smallest obligations first. The goal is to swiftly pay off smaller debts to generate motivation and momentum. This is how it works:

- **LIST DEBTS FROM SMALLEST TO LARGEST:** Start by organizing your debts in ascending order based on the outstanding balance.
- **MINIMUM PAYMENTS ON ALL DEBTS:** Continue making minimum payments on all your debts.
- **EXTRA PAYMENTS ON THE SMALLEST DEBT:** Allocate any additional funds you have for debt repayment to the smallest

debt. Once the smallest debt is paid off, roll over the amount you were paying on it to the next smallest debt.

- **REPEAT UNTIL DEBT-FREE:** Repeat this process until you've paid off all your debts. As each debt is paid off, the amount available for repayment grows, creating a snowball effect.

The Snowball method is praised for its psychological benefits. The quick wins of paying off smaller debts provide a sense of accomplishment and motivation to tackle larger debts.

2. **AVALANCHE METHOD:**

In contrast, the Avalanche method ranks debts according to their interest rates. In order to reduce the overall interest paid over time, it prioritizes paying off the debt with the highest interest rate first. This is a detailed explanation of the Avalanche method:

- **LIST DEBTS BY INTEREST RATE**: Your debts should be arranged from highest to lowest interest rate in descending order.
- **MINIMUM PAYMENTS ON ALL DEBTS:** Like the Snowball method, continue making minimum payments on all your debts.
- **EXTRA PAYMENTS ON THE HIGHEST INTEREST DEBT:** Any extra money should

go toward the debt with the highest interest rate. Transfer the money to the next highest-interest debt after that one has been paid off.

- **REPEAT UNTIL DEBT-FREE:** Continue this process until you've paid off all your debts. The Avalanche method is designed to minimize the overall interest paid and helps you become debt-free faster.

COMPARISON:

The *Snowball* method prioritizes psychology, aiming to build motivation through small victories, while the *Avalanche* method focuses on financial efficiency by tackling high-interest debts first. The choice between the two depends on individual preferences, financial goals, and psychological factors.

6.5 NEGOTIATING LOWER INTEREST RATES

Negotiating lower interest rates can be a strategic and financially prudent move for individuals seeking to manage their debt more effectively. Whether you're dealing with credit card debt, a mortgage, or a personal loan, taking proactive steps to secure lower interest rates can save you money in the long run. Here are some tips to guide you through the negotiation process.

Firstly, it is essential to understand your current financial situation and creditworthiness. Borrowers with high credit scores are usually eligible for lower interest rates from lenders. Obtain a copy of your credit report, review it for accuracy, and take appropriate action to improve your credit score if necessary. This may mean paying off any outstanding debt, making on-time bill payments, and correcting any errors on your credit report.

Once you have a clear picture of your financial standing, research the current interest rates in the market. Having this knowledge provides you with a benchmark and empowers you during negotiations. If you find that other lenders are offering better rates, use this information as leverage when discussing terms with your current lender.

Next, contact your lender and express your desire to negotiate for lower interest rates. Be prepared to articulate why you believe you deserve a rate reduction. Highlighting your positive payment history, loyalty as a customer, and improved credit score can strengthen your case. Emphasize your commitment to meeting your financial obligations and how a lower interest rate would make it easier for you to do so.

It is important to be polite and professional during negotiations. Avoid making demands or threats, as this may be counterproductive. Instead, frame the conversation as a collaborative effort to find a solution that benefits both parties. Lenders are often willing to work with responsible borrowers who are facing temporary financial challenges.

If your lender seems hesitant to lower your interest rate, feel free to explore other options. Competition among financial institutions can work in your favor. Obtain quotes from different lenders and use these offers as leverage to negotiate with your current lender. Be transparent about the rates you've been offered elsewhere, emphasizing your preference to maintain a positive relationship but indicating your willingness to switch if necessary.

Unexpected life events, such as serious illnesses or accidents, can lead to high medical expenses that aren't covered by the government or employment health insurance. It is important to recognize that even the most disciplined individuals can face financial hardships due to unforeseen circumstances, emphasizing the importance of emergency funds and insurance coverage.

We acknowledge that not everyone has access to the same financial services and education. For some, there are barriers to entry, or it may be more difficult to access resources to assist with a debt reduction plan. Research government or local services to see if there are avenues to explore. Advocate for improved financial education and accessibility to financial services.

There is also the issue of corporate practices, such as predatory lending or exploitative financial products. Individuals may face challenges not only due to personal decisions but also as a result of financial systems that may only sometimes act in the best interest of consumers.

After much discussion, John and Jane decide on a debt reduction plan that they believe is best for the family and their journey to financial empowerment. They adjust their budget accordingly.

John and Jane understand that debt serves as a tool for financial growth, but can lead to instability if mishandled. They pay close attention to the different types of debt they have, their impact, and strategies for repayment. They prioritize high-interest debts, adjust their budget, and seek lower interest rates as key steps to manage and eliminate the debt effectively.

7

BUILDING AND MAINTAINING GOOD CREDIT

As hard as it is, John has been following their plan for debt reduction to the letter. He notices that there has been a significant improvement in their credit score as of late. John can now appreciate how important it is to pay off debt and have good credit.

One of the most important aspects of personal financial management is establishing and preserving good credit. Having a clean credit history can help you take advantage of many financial opportunities, including getting loans, getting good interest rates, and even getting the upper hand when potential employers are doing background checks. To maintain a good credit profile, you should follow certain rules and adopt responsible financial habits.

The first step in establishing good credit is under-standing the fundamentals of credit reporting. Your credit report has details about your credit accounts, past due amounts, balances owed, and any nega-tive marks like late or default payments that may be present. It also represents your credit history. You can identify errors, monitor your progress, and take prompt action to address any issues by regularly reviewing your credit report.

The cornerstone of a healthy credit history is timely payment of bills. Consistently paying credit card bills, loans, and other obligations by their due dates demonstrates financial responsibility to creditors. Late payments not only result in fees and increased interest rates, they also negatively impact your credit score. To ensure timely payments and prevent errors, it can be very helpful to set up automatic pay-ments or reminders.

Diversifying your credit portfolio is another effective strategy for building good credit. Although a variety of credit types, including retail accounts, credit cards, and installment loans, can raise your credit score, it is important to handle them carefully. Opening new credit accounts should be done cautiously, as multi-ple inquiries within a short period can temporarily lower your score.

A good credit rating requires maintaining a low credit usage ratio. This ratio shows you how much of your available credit you are currently using. This tells creditors that you can handle your money and aren't unduly dependent on credit. It is usually advised to keep this ratio below 30 percent.

Monitoring your credit score is essential to tracking your development and identifying possible areas for improvement.

Because so many financial institutions and credit card companies offer free access to credit scores, customers can easily monitor their credit. Early detection of negative trends allows you to take action before they worsen.

In the event of financial challenges, communication with creditors is key. If you anticipate difficulties in meeting payment obligations, contacting your creditors proactively and exploring potential solutions, such as payment plans or temporary hardship arrangements, can mitigate the impact on your credit score. Ignoring financial issues may lead to more severe consequences, such as collections or charge-offs, which can damage your credit history significantly.

It takes time to establish and preserve good credit, and it requires diligence and prudent money management. You can build a solid credit foundation that will help you in many areas of your financial life by keeping up with your credit profile, paying your bills on time, diversifying your credit, and managing your credit responsibly. In the end, having a good credit history gives you access to financial opportunities and a strong base on which to build your long-term financial objectives.

7.1 THE IMPORTANCE OF A STRONG CREDIT SCORE

An important financial asset that has a big impact on many different areas of a person's financial life is a high credit score. It is a critical component that lenders take into account when assessing loan applications and acts as a numerical representation of a person's creditworthiness. Here are a few main points about how crucial it is to keep your credit score high.

1. **ACCESS TO CREDIT:**
   An excellent credit score makes it possible for you to take advantage of many different credit opportunities. Whether you're applying for an auto loan, mortgage, credit card, or other type of loan, to determine your credit risk, lenders look at your credit score. A high credit score makes it more likely that you will be approved and gives you access to credit on more favorable terms, such as lower interest rates.

2. **LOWER INTEREST RATES:**
   Being able to obtain loans at reduced interest rates is one of the key advantages of having a high credit score. Higher credit scores qualify borrowers for more favorable interest rates because lenders view them as lower risk.

3. **CREDIT CARD APPROVAL AND LIMITS**:
   Credit card companies often reserve the most attractive offers for individuals with strong credit scores. The likelihood of getting approved for premium credit cards with superior benefits and rewards is higher for those with higher credit scores. Additionally, it can lead to higher credit limits, providing more financial flexibility.

4. **INSURANCE PREMIUMS:**
   Credit scores are sometimes used by insurance companies to set rates for homeowners and auto insurance. Strong credit may help you save money on insurance because insurers think customers with better credit scores are less likely to make claims.

5. **EMPLOYMENT OPPORTUNITIES:**
   When hiring new employees, some companies take credit history into account, particularly when the role involves financial responsibilities. While this practice is not universal, maintaining a strong credit score can be advantageous for job seekers in industries where financial integrity is a key consideration.

6. **RENTING A HOME:**
   Credit scores are a common tool used by property management firms and landlords to assess potential tenants. More favorable rental terms and a higher chance of approval for a rental property can result from having a higher credit score.

7. **UTILITY DEPOSITS:**
   Some utility companies may require security deposits from individuals with lower credit scores. A strong credit history can help you avoid or reduce these deposits, saving you money and making it easier to establish utility services.

8. **FINANCIAL SECURITY AND PEACE OF MIND:**
   A strong credit score reflects responsible financial behavior and management. It provides a sense of financial security and peace of mind, knowing that you can access credit when needed and on favorable terms. This can be especially crucial during unexpected financial emergencies.

7.2 TIPS FOR IMPROVING AND MAINTAINING CREDIT HEALTH

From getting a loan to determining interest rates, your credit score affects many facets of your financial life. Paying close attention to your spending patterns and managing your credit responsibly is essential to maintaining and raising your credit score. The following are some crucial pointers to help you keep and improve a positive credit profile:

1. **REGULARLY REVIEW YOUR CREDIT REPORT TO LOOK FOR AND FIX ERRORS:**
   Regularly review your credit report from all three major credit bureaus – Equifax, Experian, and TransUnion. Verify the accuracy of the information and raise any inaccuracies you come across. To keep your credit history current and dependable, you must take this action.
2. **PAY BILLS ON TIME:**
   One of the biggest things influencing your credit score is timely payments. To help you remember when things are due, set up automated payments or reminders. On-time payments on a regular basis show financial responsibility and enhance your creditworthiness.
3. **REDUCE CREDIT CARD BALANCES:**
   Your credit score may need to be improved if you have high credit card balances in comparison to your credit limit. Try not to use more than 30 percent of your credit limit. Your credit score can rise, and your interest costs can go down when you pay off balances.
4. **DIVERSIFY YOUR CREDIT MIX:**
   Having multiple credit products, including installment loans, mortgages, and credit cards, can improve your credit score. However, only

open new credit accounts when necessary, as having too many inquiries in a short period can hurt your credit score.

5. **AVOID CLOSING OLD CREDIT ACCOUNTS:**
The length of your credit history has an impact on your credit score. Your credit history is shortened when you close old credit accounts, which could result in a lower credit score. Keep your oldest accounts open and make responsible use of them to show that you have a solid credit history.

6. **CREATE A REALISTIC BUDGET:**
Develop a budget to manage your finances effectively. Knowing your income, expenses, and spending habits helps you avoid overspending, late payments, and accumulating unnecessary debt. A well-managed budget contributes to financial stability.

7. **EMERGENCY FUND:**
An emergency fund can shield you from unexpected expenses that could result in late payments or higher credit card debt. To ensure financial security, try to save three to six months' worth of living expenses.

8. **NEGOTIATE WITH CREDITORS:**
If you're facing financial challenges, reach out to your creditors to discuss your situation. They may offer temporary relief, such as lower interest rates or modified payment plans, to help you manage your debts without damaging your credit further.

9. **EDUCATE YOURSELF:**
   Stay informed about credit management and financial literacy. Understanding how credit scores are calculated and the factors that influence them empowers you to make informed decisions that have a positive impact on your credit score.

10. **USE CREDIT WISELY:**
    Be strategic when applying for credit. Only open a few accounts, and only apply for credit when it is necessary. Using credit responsibly enhances your creditworthiness and shows financial responsibility.

John and Jane want to celebrate each milestone in their financial journey. They have been working hard to follow their plan to the letter. Although they still have more debt to pay off, they recently paid off one of their highest interest rate credit cards.

They have now come to John's favorite part of the process... celebrating. To celebrate this milestone in their financial journey, John decides to get that grill he wanted and Jane decides to upgrade her yoga class subscription to Gold-Tier. Thank goodness they budgeted for these beforehand.

Establishing and maintaining good credit is crucial for financial success. A clean credit history opens doors to loans, better interest rates, and job opportu-

nities. Timely payments, diverse credit, and regular monitoring are key. A strong credit score provides access to credit, lowers rates, and fosters financial security and peace of mind.

8

EXPLORING ADDITIONAL INCOME STREAMS

Jane is a 'want-trepreneur.' She likes to try her hand at new business ventures and is always turning her hobbies into side hustles. She is looking for ways to bring in additional income streams. John is always there to help.

The idea of depending only on one source of income is becoming less and less common in today's dynamic and constantly shifting economic environment. A growing number of people are realizing how important it is to diversify their sources of income to improve their financial security and stability. In order to manage uncertainty, accomplish financial objectives, and build a more robust financial portfolio, investigating alternative sources of income has evolved into a calculated strategy.

The need for more financial flexibility is one of the main drivers of the search for new revenue sources. Having a variety of sources of income protects against unanticipated expenses, economic down-turns, and sudden job losses. It provides peace of mind and serves as a safety net by easing financial strain. Furthermore, having a variety of income sources enables people to invest in opportunities, manage their money wisely, and establish a stronger financial base.

Several avenues can be explored to generate additional income, depending on one's skills, interests, and available resources. Freelancing is a popular option, enabling individuals to leverage their expertise in various fields, such as writing, graphic design, programming, or marketing. Numerous opportunities exist for connecting freelancers with clients through online platforms, which offer a convenient and adaptable means of earning additional income.

Investing is another avenue for creating additional income streams. Whether it is in stocks, bonds, real estate, or other financial instruments, investing can generate passive income over time. Passive income builds up without requiring active participation. Examples include dividends, interest, and rental income. A certain amount of risk is always associated with investing, but possible drawbacks can be reduced with careful planning and research.

The gig economy has seen significant growth, offering numerous opportunities for individuals to earn income on a part-time or temporary basis. Ridesharing, food delivery, and short-term rentals are just a few examples of gig economy activities that can be pursued alongside a primary job. These flexible opportunities cater to diverse skills and preferences, allowing individuals to choose options that align with their lifestyles.

Entrepreneurship is yet another avenue to explore when looking to diversify income streams. Starting a small business or side hustle allows individuals to capitalize on their passion and skills. Whether it is selling handmade crafts, offering consulting services, or launching an online store, entrepreneurship provides a platform to turn hobbies into income-generating ventures.

Moreover, the digital era has opened up avenues for creating content and monetizing it through various platforms. Blogging, podcasting, YouTube channels, and social media can be effective mediums for sharing knowledge, experiences, or entertainment while earning revenue through advertisements, sponsorships, or affiliate marketing.

While the prospect of exploring additional income streams is enticing, it is crucial to approach it with a well-defined plan. Time management becomes paramount as you balance your primary responsibilities with new income-generating activities. Setting realistic goals, identifying sustainable opportunities, and continuously assessing and adjusting the strategy are essential components of a successful income diversification plan.

8.1 INCOME ENHANCEMENT STRATEGIES

Income enhancement strategies refer to a set of proactive measures you can adopt to increase your earnings and improve your overall financial well-being. These tactics cover a range of areas related to investment, money management, and both professional and personal development. Implementing these strategies requires a combination of discipline, creativity, and a long-term perspective. Here are some key income enhancement strategies:

1. **INVEST IN EDUCATION AND SKILL DEVELOPMENT:**
    Developing new skills and continuing education are essential for being competitive in today's fast-paced labor market. Gaining certifications, going to workshops, and investing in education can lead to higher-paying jobs.

Putting money into your education and skill development will have a big impact on your ability to make money. Maintaining current knowledge of industry trends and engaging in ongoing education improves your marketability and increases your competitiveness in the job market. Acquiring new qualifications or abilities can help you advance in your career and land better-paying positions, in addition to increasing your value to employers.

2. **NEGOTIATE AND ADVOCATE FOR YOURSELF:**
When entering a new job, during performance reviews, or when seeking a raise, be prepared to articulate your value to the organization. Research industry standards, highlight your accomplishments, and negotiate your compensation package confidently. Remember not to underestimate the power of negotiation. If you're a freelancer or contractor, be proactive in negotiating your rates. With increased experience and a solid portfolio, you will be able to charge more for your services. Regularly review your performance and seek opportunities for advancement within your current role or elsewhere.

3. **CREATE MULTIPLE REVENUE STREAMS:**
Consider building multiple revenue streams by leveraging your skills and expertise. This could include consulting, teaching, writing, or

starting a side business. These ventures can supplement your primary income and offer financial security. Diversifying your sources of income is a good way to optimize your current income. Investigate other sources of income, such as part-time jobs, freelancing, or passive investments. Overall earnings can rise, and stability can be achieved through diversification. You may be more susceptible to unforeseen life events or economic downturns if you are completely dependent on one source of income. Examine side projects, independent contractor work, or investments that fit your interests and skill set. In addition to raising your earning potential, diversifying your sources of income helps you build a stronger financial foundation.

4. **FINANCIAL PLANNING AND BUDGETING:** Efficient financial management is essential. Create a realistic budget, track your expenses, and identify areas where you can save money. Allocating resources wisely can free up funds for investments or debt reduction.

5. **INVEST WISELY:** Examine investment options that fit your financial objectives and risk tolerance. With time, a well-thought-out investment strategy can bring in extra money from stocks, real estate, or other investment vehicles.

6. **NETWORKING AND RELATIONSHIP BUILDING:**
   Networking is not just about socializing—it is about building relationships that can lead to career opportunities. Participate in industry events, join professional associations, and network with like-minded individuals who may be able to offer enlightening information or opportunities for collaboration.

7. **ASSESS AND ADAPT CONTINUOUSLY:**
   The job market and economic landscape are constantly evolving. Regularly assess your skills, industry trends, and financial goals. Be willing to adapt and make necessary changes to stay ahead of the curve.

8.2 EXPLORING PASSIVE INCOME OPPORTUNITIES

The concept of passive income has grown in popularity in the ever-evolving realm of personal finance. Passive income is the money earned from activities that continuously generate income even if you are not actively participating, such as dividends earned on stocks. Passive income streams offer the freedom to pursue other interests and the allure of financial independence, unlike traditional jobs that require constant effort to generate income. Creating passive income streams is a strategic approach to financial independence that involves generating earnings with minimal ongoing effort. While it may be partially hands-on initially, the goal is to set up systems that require less and less active participation over time.

It is important to note that creating passive income streams often requires upfront effort, whether it is in the form of time, money, or both. Building a successful passive income portfolio requires careful planning, research, and ongoing management. Diversification is crucial to lowering risk and ensuring a more reliable and durable source of income. Investing is one well-liked method of generating passive income. Investment vehicles such as dividend-paying stocks, bonds, real estate, and mutual funds can produce consistent income without constant supervision. Through prudent investment selection, you can create a diversified portfolio that generates a consistent flow of passive income, taking your financial objectives and risk tolerance into account. Let's examine a few well-liked passive income options.

1. **REAL ESTATE INVESTMENTS:**
   Passive income through real estate has long been a popular option. Rent payments from rental properties can be a reliable source of income for property owners. Platforms for real estate crowdfunding have also surfaced, enabling investors to pool funds for more ambitious real estate projects and split the profits.

2. **DIVIDEND STOCKS:**
   Purchasing dividend-paying stocks is a dependable way to generate passive income. A lot of well-established businesses pay dividends to their shareholders from a portion of their profits. These dividends have the potential to compound over time and offer a reliable source of income without requiring constant market observation.

3. **PEER-TO-PEER LENDING:**
   Borrowers and individual lenders are connected through peer-to-peer lending platforms. Users can profit from interest on the loans they make by taking part in these lending platforms. Though there are risks, this approach can produce interest payments and serve as a substitute for conventional banking systems.

4. **CREATE AND SELL DIGITAL PRODUCTS:**
   In the current digital era, producing and marketing digital goods like stock photos, e-Books, and online courses can be a profitable source of side income. These products don't require constant work once they are made and can be sold again.

5. **AFFILIATE MARKETING:**
   Promoting goods or services and getting paid a commission for each sale made via your special affiliate link are the two main aspects of affiliate marketing. By endorsing products they genuinely believe in, bloggers,

YouTubers, and social media influencers frequently use affiliate marketing to make passive income.

6. **AUTOMATED ONLINE BUSINESSES:**
Building and automating online businesses, such as drop-shipping or print-on-demand services, can be a hands-off way to generate income. These businesses often rely on automated processes and third-party services to handle tasks like inventory management and order fulfillment.

7. **LICENSING INTELLECTUAL PROPERTY:**
If you possess creative talents, consider licensing your intellectual property. This could include licensing your photography for stock images, music for commercial use, or even software applications. Once licensed, you can earn royalties whenever your work is used.

8. **HIGH-YIELD SAVINGS ACCOUNTS:**
Certificates of deposit (CDs) and high-yield savings accounts can offer a steady passive income stream through interest payments, even though they are not as risky as other investment options.

8.3 REAL ESTATE AND RENTAL INCOME

Real estate investment, a cornerstone of wealth-building, encompasses a diverse array of opportunities, from residential properties to commercial ventures. The prospect of generating rental income, a key component of real estate investment, attracts investors seeking both short-term cash flow and long-term appreciation. Buying single-family homes or multi-unit buildings is a common way for investors to start their investment careers.

These assets provide a stable foundation for rental income, with tenants contributing monthly payments that cover mortgage expenses and potentially yield a surplus. The residential market, driven by factors like population growth and lifestyle changes, offers consistent demand for rental properties.

Multi-unit properties, in particular, present a unique advantage as they allow for multiple income streams from a single investment. This diversification can mitigate risks associated with vacancies or unexpected expenses. Additionally, strategic property management and improvements can enhance the overall value, leading to increased rental income and property appreciation.

Commercial real estate introduces a different dimension to rental income. Retail spaces, offices, and industrial properties cater to businesses seeking locations to operate. Lease agreements with commercial tenants often involve longer terms and higher rental rates, providing a reliable income source for investors. However, the commercial sector is sensitive to economic trends and market fluctuations, requiring a nuanced approach to investment decisions.

The emergence of platforms such as Airbnb has led to a notable expansion of the short-term rental market. Purchasing real estate in popular tourist locations or urban areas is one way for investors to profit from this trend. Although there may be more potential for profit from short-term rentals, there are also more management duties and ongoing property upkeep requirements.

The real estate market's cyclical nature influences rental income, with fluctuations in property values impacting investor returns. Savvy investors recognize the importance of timing their investments to maximize profitability. Long-term holding periods offer the benefit of both steady rental income and capital appreciation, aligning with a buy-and-hold strategy.

Effective property management plays a pivotal role in realizing the full potential of rental income. Timely repairs, responsive communication with tenants, and strategic marketing contribute to tenant

satisfaction and retention. A well-maintained property not only attracts quality tenants but also minimizes vacancies, ensuring a continuous stream of
rental income.

Successful examples abound in the ever-changing
real estate investing sector, demonstrating the need
for diversified income sources. Take the example of
astute investor Sarah Thompson, who operates out
of a developing metropolis. By purchasing both residential and commercial real estate, Sarah diversified
her real estate holdings in a calculated manner.

RESIDENTIAL INVESTMENT SUCCESS

Sarah initiated her investment journey by purchasing a single-family home in a burgeoning neighbor-
hood. Leveraging the demand for rental properties
driven by population growth and lifestyle changes,
she secured reliable tenants and enjoyed a steady
rental income. Recognizing the potential for scalability, Sarah expanded her portfolio to include
multi-unit buildings. This move not only increased
her overall rental income but also provided a safety
net against the occasional vacancy.

NAVIGATING COMMERCIAL REAL ESTATE CHALLENGES

Another example is Mike Rodriguez, who ventured
into commercial real estate. Aware of the sensitivity

of this sector to economic trends, Mike did meticulous research and selected prime locations for retail spaces and offices. His careful tenant selection and long-term lease agreements ensured a stable and higher rental income. Despite market fluctuations, Mike's strategic approach and diversification into different commercial properties allowed him to weather economic downturns and maintain a consistent income stream.

EMBRACING SHORT-TERM RENTAL TRENDS

In the era of short-term rentals, Emily Davis capitalized on the popularity of platforms like Airbnb. Purchasing a property in a sought-after tourist destination, Emily turned her investment into a lucrative short-term rental. While the demand for such accommodations offered a potential for higher profits, Emily's success story also highlights the importance of effective property management and responsive communication to maintain a positive reputation on rental platforms.

These case studies underscore the adaptability and strategic thinking required for successful real estate investment. Each investor tailored their approach based on market dynamics, risk tolerance, and long-term goals. The stories of Sarah, Mike, and Emily demonstrate the diverse opportunities within the real estate sector and how astute decisions can lead to a resilient and varied income portfolio.

Remember, these examples highlight the importance of thorough research, market analysis, and understanding local regulations, showcasing the value of a well-informed and strategic approach to real estate investment.

Tax considerations add another layer to the financial landscape of real estate investments. Deductible expenses, depreciation, and other tax advantages can optimize the after-tax returns on rental income. Investors often consult with tax professionals to navigate the intricacies of real estate taxation and maximize their overall financial position.

Despite the potential for lucrative returns, real estate investing requires careful research and due diligence. Market analysis, property inspections, and an understanding of local regulations are essential elements of a successful investment strategy. Investors must also assess their risk tolerance and financial goals to align their real estate portfolio with their broader investment objectives.

8.4 THE POWER OF DIVIDEND STOCKS AND SMART INVESTMENTS

Investors are always looking for ways to produce consistent returns and accumulate wealth over time. Investing in dividend stocks is one tactic that has proven to be successful over time. These stocks present a special opportunity since they offer dividends, which are a consistent source of income, along with the possibility of capital growth.

Dividend stocks are ownership interests in businesses that pay out dividends to shareholders from a portion of their profits. A steady cash flow for living needs, portfolio diversification, or stock reinvestment may be of particular interest to investors seeking this kind of income. Making the most out of dividend stocks requires knowledge and intelligent investing choices.

The stability dividend stocks provide to an investment portfolio is one of their main benefits. Businesses that regularly distribute dividends are frequently well-established and have a track record of steady profits. This feature can act as a buffer during market downturns because dividend income lessens the impact of possible stock price losses. This can be an essential part of a well-rounded investment strategy for income-focused investors.

Moreover, dividend-paying stocks have historically demonstrated resilience during economic downturns. Companies that prioritize returning value to shareholders through dividends are often more disciplined in managing their finances. This financial prudence can make these companies better equipped to weather economic challenges and emerge stronger on the other side. As a result, dividend stocks can act as a defensive play, offering a degree of protection during market volatility.

Investors need to do thorough research before diving into the world of dividend stocks. Not all high-dividend-yield stocks are created equal, and a high yield may sometimes signal underlying risks. Analyzing a company's financial health, dividend history, and payout ratio is crucial to assess the sustainability of its dividend payments.

Another essential component of successful investing is diversification, and dividend stocks can be a major component of a portfolio that is well-diversified. Investors can spread risk and lessen the effects of underwhelming performance in any one sector by making investments in businesses from other sectors and industries. This strategy aids in creating a robust portfolio that can withstand a range of market circumstances.

In addition to individual stocks, there are investment vehicles such as dividend-focused exchange-traded funds (ETFs) that offer exposure to a diversified basket of dividend-paying companies. These funds provide a convenient way for investors to gain access to a broad spectrum of dividend stocks without having to pick individual stocks themselves.

Diversifying income streams is crucial for financial security. Options include freelancing, investing, gig economy work, entrepreneurship, content creation, and passive income avenues like real estate or dividend stocks. Strategic planning and ongoing assessment are key.

9

NAVIGATING FINANCIAL CHALLENGES

Jane's mother Martha was in a car accident and the medical bills are through the roof. How can John and Jane adapt to this sudden financial challenge?

Financial difficulties appear as strong threads that entwine the complex tapestry of life. These difficulties, which can arise from unanticipated events, economic downturns, or personal decisions, can have a negative impact on our wellbeing. But financial instability also presents a chance for fortitude, development, and a revitalized sense of financial empowerment.

One of the initial steps in navigating financial challenges is cultivating a mindset of adaptability. The landscape of personal finance is dynamic, subject to both macroeconomic shifts and individual circumstances. Accepting the fluidity of financial situations allows individuals to approach challenges with a sense of pragmatism and openness to change. This mindset shift can be transformative, fostering creative problem-solving and encouraging a proactive stance in facing financial hurdles.

In times of financial strain, communication becomes a vital tool. Sharing concerns and collaborating with family members, friends, or financial advisors can illuminate potential solutions and alleviate the burden of isolation. A collective effort often leads to innovative strategies and a shared sense of responsibility, reinforcing the idea that overcoming financial challenges is a collaborative journey.

Moreover, exploring supplemental income streams can be a proactive strategy to bolster financial stability. In the gig economy era, opportunities for freelancing, consulting, or part-time work abound. Having a variety of sources of income not only helps one stay afloat financially but also develops important skills that expand one's career options. Financial difficulties can become opportunities for both professional and personal development if you embrace the gig economy.

Financial literacy is the cornerstone of navigating challenges successfully. Understanding the nuances of investments, debt management, and savings instruments empowers individuals to make informed decisions. Financial counseling services, workshops, and educational materials can give people the skills they need to handle complicated financial situations. One is better able to make strategic decisions that support their long-term financial goals when they are well-informed.

In the face of financial challenges, embracing a frugal lifestyle can be a temporary yet impactful measure. Differentiating between wants and needs and curbing unnecessary expenditures can free up resources to address pressing financial concerns. This conscious approach to spending not only alleviates immediate financial strain but also cultivates a sustainable and mindful relationship with money.

The process of overcoming financial obstacles requires resourcefulness and resiliency. Despite their potential for hardship, challenges can also be powerful drivers of both financial and personal development. Individuals can turn financial challenges into opportunities for long-lasting positive change by prioritizing financial literacy, embracing communication, fostering adaptability, diversifying income, and adopting a frugal mindset. These difficulties become threads in the life tapestry that, when woven carefully, strengthen and fortify the financial fabric.

9.1 DEALING WITH UNEXPECTED EXPENSES

Life is full of surprises, and not all of them are pleasant. One of the most challenging surprises anyone can face is an unexpected expense. Whether it is a sudden medical bill, a car repair, or a home appliance breaking down, these unforeseen costs can throw off even the most carefully crafted budgets. However, there are proactive steps you can take to navigate these financial challenges and minimize their impact on your overall financial well-being.

It is crucial to have an emergency fund. Setting aside money for unexpected expenses might sound like common advice, but it is a fundamental principle of financial planning. Your goal should be to have three to six months' worth of living expenses saved up in a convenient account. As a safety net for your finances, this emergency fund ensures that you won't have to use credit cards or loans in an emergency and shields you from unanticipated costs.

If you do not currently have an emergency fund, consider reviewing your spending to find places where you can make savings and set aside money to begin creating one. It may require making temporary sacrifices, but the peace of mind that comes with having a financial cushion is well worth the effort. When faced with an unexpected expense, resist the urge to panic. Breathe deeply and calmly evaluate the circumstances. Sort your expenses into categories according to importance and urgency. While some expenses can be postponed or negotiated, others need to be addressed right away. For example, if you're hit with a medical bill, contact the healthcare provider to discuss payment plans or potential discounts.

Explore alternative sources of funding. If your emergency fund is insufficient, consider borrowing from friends or family, but do so with caution and clear communication about repayment terms. Additionally, some employers offer salary advances or financial assistance programs for employees facing unexpected hardships. It is worth exploring these options before resorting to high-interest loans or credit cards.

If the unexpected expense is related to a specific asset, such as a car or home repair, research whether warranties, insurance policies, or service agreements can help cover the costs. Understanding the terms and conditions of these agreements can save you money in the long run.

In the aftermath of dealing with an unexpected expense, take the opportunity to reassess and strengthen your financial resilience. Use the experience as motivation to bolster your emergency fund and revisit your budget to identify areas for improvement. To create a more comprehensive financial plan that takes future uncertainties into account, consider speaking with a financial advisor.

Let's now look at real-life examples involving Jane and John to illustrate the importance of an emergency fund and proactive financial planning:

Over the life of their financial empowerment journey, John and Jane encounter a number of financial challenges and unexpected expenses. Here are some examples of some of the challenges, in addition to the medical bills encountered when Jane's mother had her accident.

JANE'S LESSON IN THE POWER OF AN EMERGENCY FUND:

Jane found herself in a tight spot when her car unexpectedly broke down. She initially considered using her credit card to cover the repair costs as this had always been her go to reaction. However, John reminds her of what they have learned so far in their financial journey. Jane decides to tap into their diligently maintained emergency fund. This cushion not only spares them from accumulating credit card debt but also provides a sense of financial security during an otherwise stressful situation.

JOHN'S LESSON IN PROACTIVE FINANCIAL PLANNING:

John notices that a major home appliance is suddenly in need of repair. Instead of panicking, he calmly assessed the situation and realized the importance of proactive financial planning. Having already established an emergency fund, John was able to cover the unexpected expense without jeopardizing his family's overall financial stability. This experience motivates him to regularly review the family's budget, identify areas for improvement, and contribute consistently to their emergency fund to prepare for future uncertainties.

In both Jane and John's cases, having an emergency fund served as a crucial safety net, shielding them from the need to resort to high-interest loans or credit cards. Their stories highlight the practical benefits of maintaining a financial cushion and making it an integral part of one's financial strategy.

If you currently find yourself without an emergency fund, consider following Jane and John's example. Review your spending, make temporary sacrifices, and start setting aside money to create your safety net. The peace of mind that comes from having a financial cushion is well worth the effort and can make all the difference when life throws unexpected challenges your way.

Remember, it is not just about weathering the storm, but also about using these experiences to reassess and strengthen your financial resilience. After dealing with an unexpected expense, take the opportunity to bolster your emergency fund, revisit your budget, and consider seeking guidance from a financial advisor to create a more comprehensive financial plan that accounts for future uncertainties.

9.2 STRATEGIES FOR HANDLING FINANCIAL SETBACKS

Facing financial setbacks can be a challenging and stressful experience, but it is essential to approach these situations with a strategic mindset. Whether it is an unexpected major illness, job loss, or economic downturn, implementing effective strategies can help you weather the storm and emerge stronger. Here are some key strategies to consider when handling financial setbacks:

1. **ASSESS THE SITUATION:**
   Begin by conducting a thorough assessment of your financial situation. Understand the root causes of the setback, evaluate your current assets and liabilities, and identify areas where you can cut expenses. A clear understanding of your financial landscape is crucial for developing a viable recovery plan.

2. **REVIEW THE BUDGET:**
   Review your budget, taking your existing financial situation into account. Re-evaluate and sort costs into those that are necessary and those that are not, giving the former priority. Spend less on frivolous items and allocate more funds to necessities. A well-organized budget provides you with a financial roadmap when things get hard.

3. **EMERGENCY FUND USAGE:**
   This is when you should use your emergency fund wisely if you have one. The purpose of this fund is to act as a financial safety net in case of unforeseen circumstances. To make sure the fund lasts as long as possible, give priority to necessities like food, housing, and utilities.

4. **PRIORITIZE DEBT REPAYMENT:**
   Sort your debts in order of interest rate if you have any outstanding balances. Prioritizing repaying high-interest debt can help you avoid further financial hardship. Speak with creditors about hardship programs or short-term payment arrangements. Many organizations are eager to assist people who are struggling financially.

5. **EXPLORE ADDITIONAL INCOME SOURCES:**
   Seek out chances to bring in more money. This could entail working as a freelancer, taking on part-time work, or using your abilities to land consulting jobs. Increasing the vari-

ety of your sources of income will help you recover more quickly and give your finances a more secure base.

6. **NEGOTIATE WITH CREDITORS:**
   If you're struggling to meet financial obligations, proactively communicate with creditors. Many lenders are open to negotiating lower interest rates, extended payment terms, or even settling for a reduced amount. Be honest about your situation and explore mutually beneficial solutions.

7. **SEEK PROFESSIONAL ADVICE:**
   Consider speaking with credit counselors or financial advisors. These experts can offer tailored advice depending on your unique situation. They might provide advice on investing techniques, debt relief, or other financial instruments that support your objectives.

8. **INVEST IN SKILL DEVELOPMENT:**
   Use the setback as an opportunity for personal and professional growth. Invest time in developing new skills that enhance your employability or open up alternative income streams. Continuous learning can increase your resilience in the face of economic challenges.

9. **EXPLORE GOVERNMENT ASSISTANCE PROGRAMS:**
   Research and take advantage of government assistance programs that may be available in your region. These initiatives aim to support

and offer short-term assistance to people who are struggling financially.

9.3 MAINTAINING A POSITIVE MINDSET DURING CHALLENGES

Maintaining a positive mindset during challenges is essential for personal well-being and resilience. Life is inherently unpredictable, and everyone encounters obstacles at some point. The ability to approach these challenges with a positive mindset can significantly impact how we navigate and overcome them.

It is crucial to accept that challenges are a natural part of life. Instead of viewing them as insurmountable roadblocks, see them as opportunities for growth and learning. This shift in perspective allows you to reframe challenges as temporary hurdles rather than permanent setbacks.

One effective strategy for maintaining a positive mindset is to focus on what you can control. Often, challenges come with elements beyond our control, and dwelling on these aspects can lead to stress and negativity. By identifying factors within your control, you empower yourself to take proactive steps toward a solution. This feeling of agency cultivates optimism and increases your confidence in your capacity to overcome challenges.

A positive mindset also includes developing an attitude of gratitude. There are many things in our lives for which we are grateful, even in trying times. Focusing on the good things in life, no matter how small, can help you become more positive and divert your attention from problems. During difficult times, gratitude can help you stay balanced and serves as a potent counterbalance to negativity.

Self-compassion practice is also crucial. Recognize that difficulties do not make you less valuable or capable. Show yourself the same compassion and consideration that you would extend to a friend in a comparable circumstance. Recognize your efforts and accomplishments, no matter how small, and accept that obstacles are an inevitable part of the process.

Having social support is essential for keeping an optimistic outlook. Assemble a network of friends, relatives, or coworkers who are encouraging and can provide perspective. Talking to others about your struggles not only gives you emotional support but also enables you to get insightful feedback from others.

Another essential component of maintaining optimism in the face of adversity is setting reasonable goals. Divide more complex issues into smaller, more doable tasks. Reaching these smaller objectives gives you momentum and a sense of accomplishment, which helps you maintain a positive outlook. Recognize and celebrate your victories along the way to help others believe that progress is achievable even in the face of difficulty.

Techniques for mindfulness and meditation can be effective means of developing an optimistic outlook. These techniques help you with stress management, mental clarity, and staying in the moment. You can greatly improve your general well-being by setting aside a short amount of time each day to practice mindful breathing or meditation to help you center yourself. Adopt a growth mentality. Recognize that obstacles present chances for growth and learning. Consider failure as a springboard for improvement rather than something to be afraid of. Having a growth mindset makes you more resilient and encourages you to view obstacles as transient setbacks rather than immovable obstacles.

John and Jane understand that financial difficulties are common, arising from unforeseen events or personal decisions. Navigating these challenges requires adaptability, communication, diversifying income, financial literacy, and frugality. Their real-life examples illustrate the importance of an emergency fund and proactive planning and emphasize resilience and growth through setbacks.

10

LONG-TERM WEALTH PRESERVATION

Like John, Jane has noticed many improvements in their everyday life. However, she knows that financial empowerment is a long-term project and not a get rich quick scheme. As a result, she has started looking into how they can sustain their wealth for the long term...

Long-term wealth preservation is a financial strategy aimed at safeguarding and growing one's assets over an extended period. People and investors look for strategies to manage uncertainty and safeguard their financial future in a constantly shifting economic environment. Strategic investment choices, risk management, and careful financial planning are all part of this strategy.

Understanding that wealth accumulation is a marathon, not a sprint, is the fundamental component of long-term wealth preservation. It necessitates a methodical, patient approach that goes beyond transient market swings. This strategy relies heavily on diversification, which is a fundamental component of risk management. The volatility of a single asset class can be decreased by distributing investments among several asset classes, including stocks, bonds, real estate, and alternative investments.

Investors often turn to time-tested investment vehicles like blue-chip stocks and high-quality bonds for stable returns. These assets have historically demonstrated resilience during economic downturns and provided a reliable source of income. Additionally, dividend-paying stocks offer the dual benefit of potential capital appreciation and regular cash flow, contributing to long-term wealth preservation.

A good wealth preservation strategy must include actual assets like precious metals and real estate. Real estate investments can provide a steady stream of income through rental yields and potential capital growth over time. Two precious metals that provide a store of value resistant to fluctuations in the economy are gold and silver. They act as hedges against inflation and currency devaluation.

Embracing a buy-and-hold mentality is essential for long-term wealth preservation. Attempting to time the market or frequently trading assets can expose investors to unnecessary risks and transaction costs. Consistency in contributing to investment portfolios, especially through systematic investment plans (SIPs) in mutual funds, reinforces the power of compounding and aids in weathering market fluctuations.

Tax planning is another crucial aspect of preserving wealth over the long term. Tax efficiency and overall returns can be maximized by making use of tax-advantaged accounts, such as Individual Retirement Accounts. Furthermore, by reducing tax obligations, investigating tax-efficient investment strategies, such as tax-loss harvesting, can further support wealth preservation.

A comprehensive estate plan is integral to the long-term preservation of wealth. Establishing trusts, creating a will, and implementing a succession plan ensure a smooth transfer of assets to future generations, mitigating potential disputes and tax implications. Engaging with financial advisors and legal professionals to tailor an estate plan to specific family dynamics and financial goals adds an extra layer of security.

Adaptability is key in navigating the evolving financial landscape. Regularly reviewing and adjusting your wealth preservation strategy in response to changes in personal circumstances, market conditions, and economic trends ensures that the plan remains effective and aligned with long-term objectives.

10.1 ESTATE PLANNING

Making plans for the distribution of one's assets after death is known as estate planning, and it is an important but frequently disregarded component of financial management. Even though it might be difficult to think about your death, careful estate planning can bring you comfort and guarantee that your wishes are carried out. This process takes a number of legal, financial, and personal factors into account to produce an extensive plan that is customized to your particular situation.

Making a will is the foundation of estate planning. It is a legal document that outlines the distribution of your assets after your death. It enables you to name guardians for minor children, specify beneficiaries, and express any unique wishes you may have for your estate. Your wishes might not be followed if state laws decide how your assets are divided in the absence of a valid will.

Consider including a trust in your estate plan in addition to a will. An organization under law that holds and administers assets for beneficiaries is called a trust. Trusts can facilitate a smoother transfer of assets, reduce estate taxes, and eliminate probate. They offer flexibility and control over how your assets are distributed, especially if you want to stagger distributions over time or under specific conditions.

Estate planning also involves addressing potential tax implications. The estate tax is a federal tax on the transfer of a person's assets after death. Understanding the current tax laws and taking steps to minimize the impact on your estate is a key aspect of effective planning. This may involve gifting strategies, life insurance, and other financial instruments that can help reduce the overall tax burden on your estate.

Prioritizing healthcare decisions is an essential component of estate planning. With a durable power of attorney, you can choose an individual to handle healthcare choices in the event of your incapacitation. Your desires for medical care and life-sustaining therapies will determine how those treatments are administered.

To take evolving circumstances into account, you must regularly evaluate and revise your estate plan. A review of your plan should be necessary to make sure your objectives are still being realized after significant life events like marriage, divorce, having children, or obtaining major assets.

Estate planning is a very personal process, even though it includes financial and legal considerations. It is crucial to let your loved ones know what you want to prevent misunderstandings and possible arguments. Having frank and transparent discussions can help others understand your intentions and the choices you've made.

10.2 RETIREMENT PLANNING STRATEGIES

A critical component of money management is retirement planning, which calls for thoughtful analysis and calculated judgment. People are getting closer to the end of their careers, which means that creating comprehensive plans is necessary to guarantee a safe and comfortable retirement. To help people get ready for this important stage of life, here are some essential retirement planning techniques.

1. **START EARLY AND BENEFIT FROM COMPOUNDING:**
   One of the most effective retirement planning strategies is to start saving and investing early. The power of compounding allows investments to grow over time, and the earlier you begin, the more significant the impact. Even small contributions can accumulate substantial wealth over several decades.

2. **SET CLEAR GOALS AND ASSESS RETIRE-MENT NEEDS**:
   Setting definite retirement objectives is crucial. Establish your retirement lifestyle goals and calculate the costs involved. Think about things like travel, housing, healthcare, and recreational activities. Setting a specific financial goal will be easier if you have a realistic understanding of your needs.

3. **REVIEW AND ADJUST YOUR PLAN REGULARLY:**
   Circumstances change, and life is dynamic. Review your retirement plan on a regular basis to make sure it still fits your goals for your lifestyle, current financial status, and market conditions. As necessary, make the required course corrections and adjustments to your contributions and investment allocations to stay on track.

4. **DIVERSIFY YOUR INVESTMENTS:**
   Investing fundamentally relies on diversification. Divide your investments across a number of asset classes, including bonds, stocks, and property, to reduce risk. Diversification increases the likelihood of steady, long-term returns while shielding your portfolio from market volatility.

5. **TAKE ADVANTAGE OF EMPLOYER-SPONSORED RETIREMENT PLANS:**
   Plans for retirement savings and pensions are provided by many employers. Take full advan-

tage of these opportunities, especially if your employer matches contributions. Employer-sponsored plans provide tax advantages and can significantly boost your retirement savings.

6. **MAXIMIZE CONTRIBUTIONS TO TAX-ADVANTAGED ACCOUNTS:**
Contribute to tax-advantaged retirement accounts. These accounts offer tax benefits, either through tax-deferred growth or tax-free withdrawals in retirement. Maximize your contributions within legal limits to optimize your retirement savings.

7. **CONSIDER HEALTH CARE COSTS:**
Health care expenses often increase during retirement. Factor in potential medical costs, if not covered by government agencies, when estimating your retirement needs. If you want to safeguard yourself against large future healthcare costs, think about getting long-term care insurance.

8. **CREATE A SUSTAINABLE WITHDRAWAL STRATEGY:**
Plan for how you will withdraw funds during retirement to ensure that your savings last. A popular guideline is the "4% rule," which states that taking out four percent of your savings each year strikes a fair balance between income and capital preservation.

9. **EXPLORE ADDITIONAL INCOME STREAMS:** Investigate opportunities for additional income streams during retirement. This could include part-time work, rental income, or dividends from investments. Supplementing your retirement income can provide added financial security.

10. **SEEK PROFESSIONAL ADVICE:** Consult with financial advisors or retirement planning experts to tailor a strategy that suits your specific circumstances. Experts can offer specific guidance according to your time horizon, risk tolerance, and financial objectives.

Long-term wealth preservation involves strategic investment choices, risk management, and diversification. John and Jane prioritize stability with assets like blue-chip stocks, bonds, real estate, and precious metals. They maintain a buy-and-hold mentality, ensure financial security with tax planning, estate planning, and adaptability. They plan for retirement, emphasizing early saving, clear goals, diversification, tax-advantaged accounts, and seek professional advice for a comfortable retirement.

11

LEVERAGING TECHNOLOGY FOR FINANCIAL SUCCESS

John may be a math wiz, but he is not comfortable with all this technology stuff. Jane, on the other hand, is fascinated by technology and wants to learn more about how she can use technology to enhance their financial situation.

Leveraging technology is not just a choice in the fast-paced world of modern finance—it is a strategic necessity for achieving financial success. The intersection of finance and technology has opened new avenues for individuals and businesses to manage, grow, and protect their wealth. From digital banking to sophisticated investment platforms, technological advancements have reshaped the financial landscape, providing unprecedented opportunities for those who are savvy enough to harness their potential.

One of the most transformative aspects of technology in finance is the advent of online banking. Gone are the days of long queues and cumbersome paperwork. Today, individuals can manage their finances with a few taps on their smartphones. Online banking not only offers the convenience of access anytime, anywhere but also provides a real-time view of one's financial standing. Budgeting, tracking expenses, and setting financial goals have become seamless tasks with the help of intuitive mobile applications.

The rise of fintech platforms has democratized access to sophisticated financial tools. Robo-advisors, for instance, use algorithms to provide automated, low-cost investment advice tailored to individual risk preferences. This empowers even novice investors to make informed decisions without the need for an extensive financial background. Furthermore, artificial intelligence and machine learning algorithms analyze market trends and identify investment opportunities, enabling users to optimize their portfolios for maximum returns. Cryptocurrencies and blockchain technology have disrupted traditional notions of currency and financial transactions.

The concept of decentralized finance takes technology a step further by providing financial services like lending, borrowing, and trading without traditional intermediaries. Through smart contracts, individuals can participate in decentralized lending protocols, earning interest on their assets or obtaining loans without the need for a traditional bank. For people who don't have access to traditional banking services in particular, this creates new opportunities for financial inclusion.

Artificial intelligence (AI) is critical to risk management and fraud detection in the financial sector. Financial institutions can detect patterns and anomalies in large datasets and take proactive measures to mitigate potential risks by using sophisticated algorithms. This enhances the security of financial transactions while also supporting the general stability of the financial system.

New difficulties accompany the tremendous advantages of technology in finance. Cybersecurity risks are a result of the digital age, and people and organizations need to be cautious about safeguarding their financial data. Furthermore, because technology is changing so quickly, it is necessary to learn new things and adjust to new opportunities continuously.

11.1 INVESTMENT PLATFORMS AND ROBO-ADVISORS

For those looking to increase their wealth through automated and strategic investing methods, investment platforms and robo-advisors have become well-liked resources. Users can access the financial markets, manage their portfolios, and accomplish their investment objectives more effectively and conveniently thanks to these cutting-edge financial technologies.

INVESTMENT PLATFORMS:

Investment platforms serve as comprehensive online hubs where investors can buy, sell, and manage various financial instruments. Many investment options are available on these platforms, such as stocks, bonds, exchange-traded funds (ETFs), and more. Investors have flexibility and convenience as they can access these platforms via desktop or mobile applications.

The user interface of investment platforms is a crucial component that is intended to be simple to use and intuitive. This makes it simple for both inexperienced and seasoned investors to use the platform. Investors are capable of gathering information, examining market patterns, and deciding on their investment portfolios. Furthermore, a lot of investing platforms provide tutorials, videos, and articles as educational tools to help users improve their financial literacy.

Investment platforms often provide tools for portfolio diversification and risk management. Investors can create diversified portfolios by allocating their funds across different asset classes and industries. Some platforms also offer risk assessment tools that help investors understand their risk tolerance and make investment decisions aligned with their financial goals.

Investment platforms may cater to various investment styles, from long-term buy-and-hold strategies to more active trading approaches. Some platforms offer commission-free trading, reducing costs for investors and encouraging more frequent trading.

ROBO-ADVISORS:

A subset of investing platforms known as "robo-advisors" use algorithms and artificial intelligence to make investing decisions automatically. These digital platforms evaluate risk profiles, create and manage diversified portfolios for users, and analyze market data using algorithms. The automation feature is especially useful for people who prefer to manage their investments in a hands-off manner.

One notable advantage of robo-advisors is their ability to provide low-cost investment solutions. These platforms, in comparison to traditional financial advisors, often have lower fees because they automate the investment process. Because of its affordability, investing is now more accessible to a wider group of people.

Robo-advisors typically begin by collecting information from investors about their financial goals, risk tolerance, and investment preferences. Based on this information, the algorithms create and adjust portfolios over time, aiming to optimize returns while managing risk. Automatic rebalancing ensures that the portfolio stays aligned with the investor's goals, especially during market fluctuations.

Robo-advisors offer a high level of transparency, providing users with real-time performance data and detailed insights into their portfolios. Investors are able to monitor their investments and understand how their money is being managed thanks to this transparency.

11.2 CRYPTOCURRENCY AND BLOCKCHAIN

Blockchain technology and cryptocurrencies have come to be seen as revolutionary forces that are changing the ways we think about and carry out financial transactions. These innovations, which emerged from the need for a secure and decentralized system, have the power to drastically alter sectors of the economy that go beyond finance.

Blockchain, a distributed ledger technology that guarantees immutability, security, and transparency, is at the center of this revolution. A blockchain functions on a decentralized network of nodes, in contrast to conventional centralized systems, where a single entity controls the entire network. A copy of the ledger is kept on each node, and transactions are verified and recorded using consensus algorithms. This greatly lowers the possibility of fraud and manipulation, in addition to doing away with the need for intermediaries.

Blockchain-powered digital currencies that protect transactions and regulate the creation of new units are known as cryptocurrencies. Examples include Bitcoin and Ethereum.

An electronic cash system that operates peer-to-peer and does not rely on a central authority, like a bank, was first introduced by the industry pioneer Bitcoin. By introducing smart contracts—self-executing contracts with the terms of the agreement written directly into the code—Ethereum, on the other hand, increased the potential of blockchain technology.

The decentralized nature of cryptocurrencies brings financial inclusion to the forefront. Millions of unbanked individuals worldwide can now access financial services through their smartphones, opening up new economic opportunities. Additionally, the elimination of traditional banking intermediaries reduces transaction costs and processing times, making cross-border transactions faster and more affordable.

Blockchain technology extends beyond cryptocur-rencies, finding applications in various industries. Supply chain management, healthcare, and voting systems are just a few examples where blockchain's transparency and immutability can enhance effi-ciency and security. Blockchain lowers the possi-bility of fraud by fostering trust among participants and offering a tamper-proof record of transactions.

But problems still exist. Issues with scalability, energy consumption, and the regulatory environ-ment hamper the broad use of blockchain technology and cryptocurrencies. Mining, the energy-intensive process of transaction validation, has come under fire for its effects on the environment. Sustainable mining methods and more energy-efficient consen-sus processes are being developed in an effort to ease these concerns.

The regulatory landscape is changing to take crypto-currencies' increasing sway into account. One chal-lenge that governments and financial institutions must meet is regulating these decentralized systems while maintaining a balance between the need for innovation and consumer protection.

Maintaining the proper equilibrium will be essential to the growth of the blockchain ecosystem and cryp-tocurrencies in the future.

Increased efficiency, better access to financial services, and convenience are only a few advantages of the financial technology (fintech) industry's rapid expansion and adoption. However, these advancements also raise ethical concerns that need to be addressed carefully. Some potential ethical concerns related to fintech include:

1. PRIVACY AND DATA SECURITY:

DATA MISUSE: Fintech companies often handle vast amounts of sensitive financial and personal information. There's a risk of data misuse, such as unauthorized access, data breaches, or the sale of personal information without informed consent.

INFORMED CONSENT: Users may need to fully understand or be aware of how their data is being used. Fintech providers need to ensure transparent and comprehensive disclosure and obtain informed consent.

2. ALGORITHMIC BIAS:

DISCRIMINATION: Fintech algorithms may inadvertently perpetuate biases present in historical data, leading to discriminatory outcomes, particularly in lending and credit scoring. This could result in unfair treatment based on race, gender, or other protected characteristics.

LACK OF TRANSPARENCY: The opacity of some algorithms makes it challenging for individuals to understand how decisions are made, potentially undermining accountability.

3. FINANCIAL INCLUSION AND ACCESSIBILITY:

EXCLUSIONARY PRACTICES: While fintech has the potential to increase financial inclusion, there is a risk of excluding certain demographics, particularly those who are digitally illiterate, lack access to technology, or face socioeconomic challenges.

DIGITAL DIVIDE: The divide between those who gain from fintech breakthroughs and those who fall behind could get wider if people have unequal access to technology and internet services.

4. REGULATORY COMPLIANCE:

COMPLIANCE CHALLENGES: Fintech innovations may outpace regulatory frameworks, creating challenges when it comes to ensuring compliance with existing laws and regulations. This can lead to potential legal and ethical issues.

5. CONSUMER PROTECTION:

TRANSPARENCY: The complexity of some fintech products and services may lead to a need for more transparency. Consumers should have clear information about fees, terms, and conditions to make informed decisions.

FRAUD AND SCAMS: The speed and anonymity provided by fintech can be exploited for fraudulent activities, posing risks to consumers who may fall victim to scams.

6. JOB DISPLACEMENT:

LABOR MARKET IMPACT: The automation and efficiency gains associated with fintech may lead to job displacement in traditional financial sectors. This prompts questions concerning the moral ramifications of how society handles employment and income inequality.

The integration of technology in finance is imperative for modern success. It offers convenience through online banking, democratizes investing via robo-advisors, and revolutionizes transactions with blockchain technologies and cryptocurrencies. However, ethical concerns, including privacy issues and algorithmic biases, must be addressed amid rapid advancements.

12

BUILDING A PERSONAL BRAND FOR CAREER ADVANCEMENT

Jane wants to build her career. As an adventurous entrepreneur, she has tons of experiences that she can draw on in this endeavor. The question is, how can she best to use her personal brand for career advancement?

In a competitive job market, standing out is essential for career advancement. One effective way to distinguish yourself is by building a strong personal brand. Your brand is a reflection of who you are, what you value, and the unique qualities you bring to the table. It goes beyond a polished resume—it encompasses your online presence, professional reputation, and the way you present yourself both in person and virtually.

Determine your passions, values, and strengths first. What distinguishes you? What are your strongest areas? Understanding these facets is imperative in creating an authentic personal brand that connects with others effectively. Think about your professional accomplishments, your skill set, and the characteristics that make you stand out from the crowd.

It is time to create an online presence after you have a firm grasp of your brand. Professionals can effectively highlight their accomplishments and skills on LinkedIn. Make a strong profile that emphasizes your background, abilities, and career path. To establish yourself as a thought leader in your field, share news, articles, and insights. Remember to include a high-quality photo and write a catchy headline that highlights your special selling point.

To establish a personal brand, one must be consistent. Make sure your offline and online personas are consistent. To meet professionals who share your interests, go to conferences, industry gatherings, and networking events. Talk to people, impart your knowledge, and show genuine interest in them. In addition to broadening your professional circle, networking offers chances for mentorship and teamwork.

Your content creation and sharing are integral parts of your brand. Create a blog, write for trade journals, or post your observations on social media. Consistent, quality content helps position you as an expert in your field and demonstrates your passion for continuous learning. Be mindful of your tone and messaging, ensuring they align with your brand.

Seek feedback from peers, mentors, and colleagues. Constructive feedback helps you refine and strengthen your brand. Act on valuable insights and be open to adapting as your career evolves. Your brand should be a dynamic and evolving representation of your professional identity.

Authenticity is a cornerstone of a strong personal brand. Be true to yourself and let your personality shine through in your interactions. People connect with authenticity, and it builds trust, an invaluable asset in any professional setting.

12.1 THE IMPORTANCE OF PERSONAL BRANDING

Personal branding has become increasingly crucial in today's dynamic and competitive world. As individuals navigate through various personal and professional landscapes, establishing a strong personal brand is essential for success. Personal branding goes beyond a mere professional resume or a

LinkedIn profile—it is about crafting and managing a distinctive identity that sets individuals apart. Here are some key reasons why personal branding is important:

1. **DIFFERENTIATION IN A COMPETITIVE LANDSCAPE:**
   In a world where competition is fierce, personal branding helps individuals stand out from the crowd. It allows one to showcase their unique qualities, skills, and experiences, setting them apart from others in their field. This differentiation is vital for career advancement and professional success.

2. **CAREER ADVANCEMENT:**
   Opportunities and career advancement can come through a strong personal brand. People with a strong and positive personal brand are more likely to be noticed by employers and clients, which facilitates career advancement.

3. **TRUST AND CREDIBILITY:**
   Building a personal brand involves creating a consistent and trustworthy image. When people perceive someone as authentic, reliable, and knowledgeable in their field, it enhances trust and credibility. Trust is a fundamental element in personal and professional relationships.

4. **NETWORKING OPPORTUNITIES:**
   An effective personal brand can attract likeminded individuals and potential collabo-

rators. Networking becomes more natural when others understand your values, expertise, and what you bring to the table. A robust personal brand can lead to meaningful connections and collaborations.

5. **ADAPTABILITY AND RESILIENCE:**
Adaptability is essential in a quickly changing professional environment. A clearly defined personal brand demonstrates a person's capacity for growth, learning, and relevance. People who exhibit resilience and a dedication to ongoing improvement are more likely to be trusted by employers and clients.

6. **INCREASED VISIBILITY:**
Using a variety of platforms and channels to highlight one's abilities and knowledge is part of developing a personal brand. Being more visible can open up bigger doors, whether it is getting noticed by colleagues in the industry or drawing in new customers for independent contractors and business owners.

7. **EFFECTIVE COMMUNICATION:**
Personal branding enhances communication skills. Knowing how to articulate one's values, achievements, and goals effectively is a key component of personal branding. This skill is invaluable in professional settings, job interviews, and when presenting oneself to potential clients.

8. **CAREER SATISFACTION:**
An individual's values and passions are in line with a clearly defined personal brand. Increased job satisfaction and a sense of career fulfillment are frequently the results of this alignment. People are more likely to find opportunities and roles that align with their true selves when they are true to their brand.

9. **CONTINUOUS LEARNING AND DEVELOPMENT:**
People are encouraged to consider their areas of strength and growth with personal branding. It encourages people to have an attitude of perpetual learning and growth as they work to improve their abilities and maintain their competitiveness in their industries.

10. **LEGACY AND LONGEVITY:**
A strong personal brand contributes to an individual's legacy. It is a lasting impression that can extend beyond their immediate career. A positive personal brand can have a long-lasting impact, influencing how others perceive and remember an individual.

12.2 ESTABLISHING AN ONLINE PRESENCE

A strong internet presence is necessary for both individuals and businesses. Establishing a robust online presence can facilitate global outreach and provide opportunities for professionals, independent contractors, and prospective entrepreneurs seeking to advance their careers. Here are some crucial actions you should take to create and improve your internet presence.

1. **BUILD A PROFESSIONAL WEBSITE:**
   The online version of your storefront is your website. People will go there first to learn more about you or your company. Take the time and make the effort to create a neat, professional, and user-friendly website. Make sure it represents your company, highlights your abilities or offerings, and is easy for users to navigate.

2. **OPTIMIZE FOR SEARCH ENGINES:**
   Effective search engine optimization, or SEO, is the key to ensuring that people can find your website. To raise your website's search engine rankings, incorporate pertinent keywords into the content, headers, and meta descriptions. Continually add new, excellent content to your website to draw in search engines and users.

3. **LEVERAGE SOCIAL MEDIA:**
   Having a strong online presence can be achieved with the help of social media platforms. Determine which channels best fit your intended audience and goals. Share interesting content frequently and create a unified brand across all of your social media

accounts. Participate in pertinent industry conversations and interact with your audience by answering messages and comments.

4. **CREATE VALUABLE CONTENT:**
Content is king in the online world. Whether it is blog posts, videos, podcasts, or social media updates, creating valuable and relevant content is essential for attracting and retaining an audience. Share your expertise, insights, and experiences to position yourself as an authority in your field.

5. **NETWORK ONLINE:**
Building relationships is a key component of establishing an online presence. Join professional groups and communities relevant to your industry. Participate in discussions, share your knowledge, and connect with peers and potential collaborators. Networking online can lead to valuable opportunities, partnerships, and collaborations.

6. **SHOWCASE YOUR PORTFOLIO:**
If you're a freelancer or professional in a creative field, having an online portfolio is crucial. Display your best work, highlight your achievements, and provide testimonials from satisfied clients or colleagues. A carefully chosen portfolio enhances credibility and clarifies your value to prospective employers or clients.

7. **MONITOR YOUR ONLINE REPUTATION:**
Maintaining a positive image requires careful management of one's online reputation.

Search online for references to, evaluations of, and remarks regarding your name or brand. Address feedback politely, regardless of whether it is positive or negative. Attendee appreciation and your commitment to providing the best experience possible are demonstrated by promptly resolving issues.

8. **STAY CONSISTENT:**

   It takes consistency to build and maintain an internet presence. To keep your branding and messaging consistent across all platforms, make frequent updates to your website and social media sites and adhere to a publishing schedule.

12.3 NETWORKING STRATEGIES FOR CAREER GROWTH

A vital component of professional development, networking is essential for both career success and advancement. Developing and maintaining business relationships can improve your career trajectory, lead to new opportunities, and provide insightful information. The following are a few successful networking techniques to promote career advancement:

1. **ONLINE NETWORKING PLATFORMS:**

   Make use of social media sites such as LinkedIn to establish connections with professionals within your field. Make a strong profile that emphasizes your abilities, successes, and goals. Engage in lively participation in pertinent groups and conversations to grow your network and keep abreast of business trends.

2. **ATTEND INDUSTRY EVENTS:**
Participate in networking events, conferences, seminars, and workshops in your field. These events offer opportunities to network with like-minded people, business executives, and possible mentors. To leave a lasting impression, have your business cards and elevator pitch ready.

3. **INFORMATIONAL INTERVIEWS:**
Conduct informational interviews with professionals whose careers you admire. This not only allows you to gain valuable insights into different career paths but also helps you expand your network. Approach these interviews with genuine curiosity and a willingness to learn.

4. **MENTORSHIP PROGRAMS:**
Seek out mentorship opportunities within your organization or industry. A mentor can help you overcome obstacles, share experiences, and offer advice. Establishing a mentor-mentee relationship can significantly impact your career growth by offering personalized advice and constructive feedback.

5. **VOLUNTEER AND JOIN COMMITTEES:**
   Get involved in industry-related volunteer work or join committees and boards. Not only does this demonstrate your commitment to your profession, but it also exposes you to a broader network of professionals who share similar interests and goals.

6. **PROFESSIONAL ASSOCIATIONS:**
   Affiliate yourself with relevant professional associations. Exclusive to their members, these organizations frequently hold conferences, networking events, and parties. As a member of these associations, you gain access to a multitude of resources tailored to your industry and build credibility.

7. **ONLINE FORUMS AND COMMUNITIES:**
   Engage in online communities and forums where experts in your field talk about pertinent subjects. Participating in conversations and offering your knowledge can help you establish a reputation in the community that will draw people to you and open doors.

8. **BUILD A PERSONAL BRAND:**
   Develop a strong personal brand that reflects your skills, values, and professional identity. Consistency in your online presence, such as a well-maintained LinkedIn profile and a professional website, can make you more memorable to those you encounter in your professional network.

9. **FOLLOW UP AND STAY CONNECTED:**
   Send thank-you notes to your contacts via personalized messages after meetings or networking events to show your appreciation for their time. Remain in touch by sharing pertinent updates, checking in on a regular basis, and lending a helping hand when you can.

10. **BE GENUINE AND RECIPROCAL:**
    Authenticity is key in networking. Be genuine in your interactions, showing a sincere interest in others. Additionally, strive to be reciprocal in your relationships by offering support and assistance to your connections, creating a mutually beneficial network.

For Jane, personal branding is paramount for her career growth. She crafts an authentic identity reflecting her values and strengths. She establishes an online presence through platforms like LinkedIn, creates valuable content, and networks consistently both online and offline. She understands that trust, differentiation, and career satisfaction stem from a strong personal brand.

13

NEGOTIATION SKILLS FOR FINANCIAL GAIN

Jane needs to negotiate new terms for one of her side gigs and John feels it is time to negotiate a salary increase. The problem is, they don't know if they have the skills required to get what they want.
John is confident and very good at holding his ground when it comes time to argue but that isn't enough on its own. Jane excels at reaching compromises, tact, and diplomacy, but that isn't enough on its own either.

By putting their heads together and exchanging their strengths, the two think they can bolster their negotiating skills. While those skills are a start, there is more to negotiation than that...

In business transactions, salary negotiations, or investment deals, the ability to negotiate is essential to making money. Those who want to maximize their financial results must learn these skills. The following are essential negotiation techniques with explanations as to how each affects financial success:

1. **PREPARATION:**
   Successful negotiators invest time in researching and understanding the context, counterparts, and market conditions. This includes studying the financial landscape, identifying potential alternatives, and being aware of the other party's positions. Thorough preparation allows negotiators to make informed decisions and increases their confidence during the negotiation process.

2. **EFFECTIVE COMMUNICATION:**
   Clear and articulate communication is fundamental to successful negotiation. The ability to express thoughts concisely, listen actively, and understand the needs of both parties fosters an environment for mutual understanding. This skill is particularly crucial in financial negotiations where complex concepts and terms are involved.

3. **EMOTIONAL INTELLIGENCE:**
   Emotional intelligence involves recognizing and managing emotions, both one's own and those of others. Being empathetic and understanding the emotional undertones of

a negotiation can lead to more constructive discussions. This skill helps negotiators navigate challenging situations and build rapport, which can impact financial outcomes positively.

4. **FLEXIBILITY:**

Negotiations rarely follow a linear path. Being adaptable to changing circumstances, unexpected challenges, or new information is key. Flexibility allows negotiators to pivot when necessary, explore alternative solutions, and find creative ways to meet both parties' interests, ultimately maximizing financial gains.

5. **PROBLEM-SOLVING:**

Negotiation is often about finding mutually beneficial solutions to problems or challenges. Strong problem-solving skills enable negotiators to identify common ground, propose innovative solutions, and overcome obstacles. In financial negotiations, the ability to think critically and devise win-win scenarios is particularly valuable.

6. **PATIENCE:**

Financial negotiations can be time-consuming and may involve multiple rounds of discussions. Patience is a virtue in this context, as rushing the process can lead to suboptimal outcomes. Negotiators who can maintain composure and persevere through extended negotiations are better positioned to secure favorable financial terms.

7. **NEGOTIATION STRATEGY:**
Developing a well-thought-out negotiation strategy is crucial. This includes setting clear objectives, determining acceptable and optimal outcomes, and understanding the negotiation style of the other party. A strategic approach helps negotiators navigate the complexities of financial discussions with purpose and precision.

8. **ASSERTIVENESS:**
Being assertive is different from being aggressive. Assertiveness involves confidently expressing one's needs and interests while respecting the concerns of the other party. In financial negotiations, balanced assertiveness ensures that negotiators advocate for their financial goals without jeopardizing their relationship with the other party.

9. **CLOSING SKILLS:**
The ability to bring negotiations to a successful close is a critical skill. This involves summarizing agreements, clarifying any outstanding issues, and securing a commitment from all parties involved. Effective closing skills are instrumental in translating negotiation efforts into tangible financial gains.

10. **CONTINUOUS LEARNING:**
Negotiation is a dynamic skill that can be honed over time. Successful negotiators are open to continuous learning, seeking feedback, and refining their approach based

on past experiences. Continued success in financial negotiations is ensured by keeping abreast of market conditions, industry trends, and changing negotiation strategies.

13.1 NEGOTIATING SALARY AND BENEFITS

Negotiating salary and benefits is a crucial aspect of the job offer process, and it requires careful consideration and strategic communication. This phase of employment discussions is an opportunity for both the employer and the candidate to reach a mutually satisfying agreement.

Having a clear understanding of your value in the market, communicating effectively, and taking a strategic approach are all necessary for navigating salary negotiations successfully. Here is a thorough guide to salary negotiation that covers important ideas, tactics, and pointers:

1. **RESEARCH AND PREPARATION:**
    Before entering negotiations, conduct thorough research on industry standards, company norms, and the specific role you're applying for. Online salary surveys, industry reports, and networking with professionals in similar roles can provide valuable insights. Understand the company's financial health,

its compensation philosophy, and the typical salary range for the position.

2. **KNOW YOUR VALUE:**

   To ascertain your market value, evaluate your experience, education, and abilities. Take into account not just the base pay but also supplementary benefits like retirement plans, stock options, bonuses, and health benefits. Acknowledge your special talents and achievements that make you stand out from the competition and quantify your contributions.

3. **TIMING IS KEY:**

   It is important to negotiate salaries at the right time. Talks should ideally wait until you are fully aware of the job requirements and the employer has indicated that they would like to hire you. Avoid discussing salary too soon during the interview process, as this could be interpreted as the main topic of discussion.

4. **EXPRESS ENTHUSIASM:**

   Communicate your excitement about the job and the company before discussing compensation. This helps create a positive atmosphere and demonstrates your genuine interest in the role, fostering a collaborative tone for negotiations.

5. **BE PREPARED TO JUSTIFY YOUR REQUEST:**

   Be ready to provide specific justifications for your request when expressing your salary expectations. Emphasize your accomplishments, experience, and relevant skills that make you the perfect candidate for the job. Give specific instances of how your contributions will benefit the organization.

6. **CONSIDER THE ENTIRE PACKAGE:**
   There is more to salary negotiations than just base pay. Examine the total package of benefits, including retirement plans, health insurance, stock options, bonuses, and other benefits. Making a single component adjustment can result in an improved package as a whole.

7. **REMAIN FLEXIBLE:**
   While it is important to have a clear idea of your worth, be open to negotiation and compromise. Consider factors such as job responsibilities, growth opportunities, and company culture when evaluating offers. Being flexible demonstrates your willingness to collaborate and find a mutually beneficial solution.

8. **PRACTICE EFFECTIVE COMMUNICATION:**
   Clearly articulate your points during negotiations. Use positive and assertive language, avoiding negativity or ultimatums. Active listening is equally important—understand the employer's perspective and be open to finding common ground.

9. **SEEK WIN-WIN SOLUTIONS:**
   Approach negotiations with a mindset of creating a win-win situation. Emphasize your commitment to contributing to the com-

pany's success and frame the discussion in terms of how your value aligns with the organization's goals.

10. **KNOW WHEN TO ACCEPT:**
Recognize when you've reached a fair and acceptable offer. If the employer meets your expectations or provides a reasonable compromise, consider accepting the offer to move forward positively.

Remember that negotiation is a two-way street. While it is important to advocate for your needs, be mindful of the employer's perspective. Demonstrate your flexibility and willingness to collaborate, fostering a positive relationship from the outset.

Once an agreement is reached, request written confirmation of the terms. This document should outline the agreed-upon salary, benefits, and any other pertinent details. This ensures transparency and provides a reference point for both parties.

13.2 NEGOTIATING BUSINESS DEALS AND CONTRACTS

Negotiating business deals and contracts is a crucial aspect of conducting successful and mutually beneficial transactions between parties. The process involves careful communication, strategic decision-making, and a clear understanding of the terms and conditions involved.

Firstly, effective negotiation requires thorough preparation. Both parties must have a comprehensive understanding of their own needs, priorities, and limits, as well as those of the other party. Researching market standards, assessing the value of goods or services, and anticipating potential challenges can enhance the negotiation process.

Clear communication is paramount during negotiations. Parties should articulate their expectations, objectives, and concerns transparently. Active listening is equally important to ensure that each party fully understands the other's perspective. Building a strong foundation for a business relationship requires trust, which can only be achieved through open and honest communication.

The negotiation process involves a series of proposals, counter-proposals, and compromises. Each party must be willing to give and take to reach a mutually satisfactory agreement. Flexibility is key, and both parties should be prepared to explore creative solutions that meet their respective needs.

Drafting contracts is the culmination of successful negotiations. A well-crafted contract should clearly outline the rights, responsibilities, and obligations of each party. It should address potential risks and contingencies, providing a framework for dispute resolution. Legal professionals are often involved in reviewing and finalizing contracts to ensure compliance with relevant laws and regulations.

Continuous evaluation and adaptability are essential in the negotiation process. As circumstances change, parties may need to revisit and update their agreements. Long-term success and a good reputation in the business community can result from a proactive approach to managing business relationships.

Negotiation skills are vital in business, from salary discussions to investment deals. Effective preparation, communication, emotional intelligence, flexibility, problem-solving, patience, strategy, assertiveness, closing skills, and continuous learning are key. In salary negotiations, research, timing, enthusiasm, justification, flexibility, and win-win solutions are crucial. Negotiating business deals requires preparation, clear communication, flexibility, and well-drafted contracts for mutually beneficial outcomes.

14

MINDSET SHIFTS FOR FINANCIAL ABUNDANCE

John and Jane have all their plans, but a huge part of achievement in Financial Empowerment is believing in their own success. Jane is up to it, but on occasion John feels a bit of pessimism setting in. How can they help each other maintain the correct mindset shifts for financial abundance?

Shifting one's mindset is a pivotal step toward achieving financial abundance. A key aspect is viewing money not as a scarce resource, but as a tool for creating the life you desire. Embrace these mindset shifts for financial abundance:

1. **ABUNDANCE MENTALITY:**
   Transition from a scarcity mindset to an abundance mentality. Instead of fearing lack, believe in the infinite possibilities for wealth creation. Understand that opportunities are abundant, and success is not limited.

2. **INVESTMENT IN YOURSELF:**
   Consider yourself your best asset. Allocate resources to education, skill development, and personal growth. Recognize that investing in yourself can yield the highest returns, both personally and financially.

3. **RISK AS AN OPPORTUNITY:**
   Rather than fearing risks, perceive them as avenues for growth. A financial advisor often emphasizes strategic risk-taking as a means to achieve substantial returns. Understand and manage risks wisely to unlock potential rewards.

4. **VALUE CREATION:**
   Shift focus from earning money to creating value. Whether in a career or business, prioritize delivering quality and solving problems. Financial abundance often follows those who contribute significantly to others.

5. **MULTIPLE INCOME STREAMS:**
   Embrace the idea of diversifying income sources. A financial advisor frequently encourages clients to explore various investment options, ensuring that financial success isn't solely dependent on one channel.

6. **LONG-TERM VISION:**
   Cultivate a long-term perspective. Successful financial planning involves setting and working towards distant goals. Patience and persistence are vital qualities to weather short-term fluctuations for long-term gains.

7. **FINANCIAL LITERACY:**
   Prioritize understanding the nuances of personal finance. A financial advisor can guide you, but taking an active interest in learning about investments, taxes, and financial strategies empowers you to make informed decisions.

8. **ABANDONING THE SCARCITY MENTALITY:**
   Recognize that there is enough wealth for everyone. Celebrate others' successes rather than viewing them as competition. Collaborate and network, understanding that collective prosperity is attainable.

Incorporating these mindset shifts, with the guidance of a financial advisor, transforms your relationship with money, paving the way for financial abundance and holistic success.

14.1 OVERCOMING LIMITING BELIEFS

A key component of both professional and personal development is overcoming limiting beliefs. These self-imposed limitations are frequently the result of self-defeating beliefs about one's value, potential, or skills. People need to confront these limiting beliefs and swap them out for empowering ones in order to overcome these restrictions.

For instance, imagine a person aspiring to become a successful financial advisor. Their limiting beliefs include doubts about their financial acumen, fear of rejection, or concerns about their ability to build a client base. To overcome these obstacles, the individual must first recognize and acknowledge these limiting beliefs.

Next, they can engage in positive self-talk and affirmations. Affirmations such as "I am a knowledgeable and capable financial advisor" or "I attract and retain clients easily" can help rewire the subconscious mind. Repetition is key to reinforcing these new beliefs.

Seeking support from mentors or peers in the financial industry is another crucial step. Getting knowledge from people who have overcome comparable obstacles can yield insightful information and increase self-assurance. Making connections with seasoned financial advisors can also extend one's horizons and lead to new opportunities.

Education and skill development play a pivotal role in overcoming limiting beliefs. Taking relevant courses, staying updated on industry trends, and continuously improving one's skills instill a sense of competence and confidence. This ongoing learning process helps dispel doubts and reinforces the belief that success is achievable.

Moreover, visualizing success is a powerful technique. Creating a vivid mental image of oneself as a thriving financial advisor, managing portfolios, and assisting clients in achieving their financial goals can inspire confidence and motivation.

14.2 IDENTIFYING AND CHALLENGING NEGATIVE MONEY MINDSETS

Identifying and challenging negative money mindsets is a crucial step toward achieving financial well-being. Individuals often harbor deep-seated beliefs about money that can significantly impact their financial decisions and behaviors. Recognizing these negative money mindsets is the first step towards fostering a healthier relationship with finances.

A financial advisor's assistance in identifying people's negative money mindsets is crucial to this process. Commonly held negative beliefs include aversion to financial planning, hesitancy to invest, and fear of scarcity. These mindsets may make it more difficult to achieve financial goals and amass wealth.

The financial advisor's role extends beyond identifying these mindsets—they also play a crucial role in challenging and reshaping them. Advisors assist clients in understanding the roots of their money beliefs and replacing them with more constructive and positive ones through open communication and focused interventions.

For instance, if a client harbors a fear of scarcity, a financial advisor may employ strategies to demonstrate the benefits of budgeting, emergency funds, and smart financial planning. By gradually shifting the client's perspective, the advisor helps them embrace a more abundant mindset.

Challenging negative money mindsets often involves educating clients about the long-term benefits of certain financial practices, such as investing for growth or establishing passive income streams. Financial advisors enable their clients to make well-informed decisions that support their financial objectives by providing them with individual guidance and useful strategies.

14.3 CULTIVATING A POSITIVE AND ABUNDANT FINANCIAL MINDSET

Cultivating a positive and abundant financial mindset is essential for achieving long-term financial success and wellbeing. To foster such a mindset, individuals can adopt several key practices and perspectives that empower them to make sound financial decisions.

Having specific financial objectives is essential. Set short- and long-term objectives, like saving for a dream vacation, buying a house, or setting up for retirement. Setting and achieving specific objectives gives people direction and a sense of purpose, which encourages responsible money management.

Regularly reviewing and adjusting these goals is equally important. Life circumstances change, and so should financial plans. This adaptability ensures that individuals stay on track and continue moving toward financial abundance.

An optimistic outlook on financial challenges is also integral. Instead of viewing setbacks as insurmountable obstacles, consider them as opportunities to learn and grow. This resilience is fundamental in navigating the inevitable ups and downs of financial life.

Crucially, seek the guidance of a financial advisor. A financial advisor serves as a knowledgeable and objective partner, offering personalized strategies to achieve financial goals. Through collaboration with a financial advisor, individuals can gain valuable insights into budgeting, investing, and overall financial planning.

Cultivating gratitude for current financial circumstances fosters a positive mindset. Reflecting on one's financial achievements, no matter how small, can shift focus away from scarcity to abundance. Appreciating what one has achieved financially creates a positive feedback loop, reinforcing a mindset of abundance.

Transitioning from a scarcity mindset to abundance mentality is pivotal for financial success. Embrace mindset shifts such as valuing self-investment, viewing risks as opportunities, and prioritizing value creation. Overcoming limiting beliefs, identifying negative money mindsets, and fostering positivity with financial goals and a financial advisor's guidance are essential steps towards achieving abundance. John and Jane support each other in maintaining a positive mindset and overcoming their challenges.

15

COMMUNITY AND COLLABORATIVE WEALTH-BUILDING

Jane and John approach their siblings about starting an investment club so they can build wealth together. The siblings have not always gotten along but they do share the same goals of financial freedom. What do they do and how can they work together to reach their financial goals?

Community and Collaborative Wealth-Building are innovative approaches that emphasize collective efforts and shared resources to create economic prosperity within a community. These models foster a sense of unity and mutual support, challenging traditional notions of individual wealth accumulation.

In Community Wealth-Building, the focus is on developing local economies through cooperative enterprises, community land trusts, and socially responsible businesses. These initiatives empower community members to participate actively in decision-making processes, ensuring that the benefits of economic growth are distributed more equitably. This model often involves establishing community-owned enterprises, such as co-ops or credit unions, where members collectively contribute to and benefit from the wealth generated.

Collaborative Wealth-Building extends the idea of shared prosperity beyond individual communities, encouraging collaboration on a larger scale. It involves partnerships between diverse stakeholders, including businesses, nonprofits, and government entities, to address economic challenges collectively. The goal of this cooperative strategy is to generate equitable and sustainable economic growth by using each member's unique strengths.

Financial advisors play a crucial role in both Community and Collaborative Wealth-Building by guiding investment strategies, financial planning, and risk management. According to these models, financial advisors serve as agents of positive change, assisting people and organizations in making well-informed choices consistent with the shared prosperity tenets. Their knowledge is crucial for negotiating the difficulties involved in distributing wealth and making sure that the gains made from teamwork are properly managed and reinvested for the benefit of society as a whole.

Advisors on finance play a critical role in assisting individuals and groups in implementing sustainable and ethical financial practices within Community and Collaborative Wealth-Building frameworks, which redefine wealth creation as a collective undertaking.

15.1 COLLABORATIVE INVESTING AND SAVINGS

Collaborative investing and saving involve pooling resources and knowledge among a group of individuals with the common goal of achieving financial growth. Unlike traditional investment approaches, collaborative strategies leverage the collective wisdom and diverse perspectives of a community to make informed financial decisions.

Financial advisors play a pivotal role in collaborative investing and savings by guiding the group through the intricacies of the financial landscape. Their expertise helps members understand risk, identify investment opportunities, and create a well-balanced portfolio that aligns with individual and collective goals. By fostering open communication, financial advisors facilitate collaborative decision-making processes, ensuring that each member's financial objectives are considered.

In this dynamic environment, members actively share insights, research, and market trends, promoting a learning community where knowledge is a collective asset. This collaborative approach not only empowers individuals with varied financial backgrounds, but also creates a supportive network for informed decision-making.

Financial advisors serve as pillars of trust and expertise, steering the group away from potential pitfalls. Their role extends beyond traditional advisory services, encompassing education and continuous support to ensure that all members are equipped with the tools they need for financial success. Through collaborative investing and savings, participants can benefit from diversified portfolios, reduced risks, and the combined knowledge of the group.

15.2 CREATING SUPPORTIVE FINANCIAL NETWORKS

For those looking to establish a stable and secure financial future, developing supportive financial networks is essential. Building solid relationships with competent financial advisors is a crucial component of these networks. These experts are crucial in helping people make a variety of financial decisions, providing them with individual guidance, and assisting them in navigating the complexities of the financial environment.

1. **BUILDING RELATIONSHIPS WITH FINANCIAL ADVISORS:**
   Establishing a solid rapport with a trusted financial advisor is fundamental. This involves researching and selecting an advisor with a proven track record, relevant expertise, and a client-centric approach. Regular communication fosters a deeper understanding of individual financial goals and enables advisors to tailor strategies accordingly.

2. **DIVERSIFYING INVESTMENTS:**
   A supportive financial network encourages diversification of investments. Financial advisors can assess risk tolerance, financial goals, and time horizons to create a well-rounded investment portfolio. Diversification minimizes risk and enhances the potential for long-term financial growth.

3. **FINANCIAL EDUCATION:**
   A robust financial network includes educational components. Financial advisors educate clients on various investment options, savings strategies, and tax implications. People who feel empowered are better equipped to make wise choices and take an active role in determining their financial destiny.

4. **REGULAR FINANCIAL CHECKUPS:**
   Just as physical health requires regular checkups, financial health benefits from periodic assessments. Financial advisors conduct reviews to ensure that financial plans align with changing circumstances, market conditions, and personal goals. Adjustments are made as needed to maintain optimal financial wellbeing.

5. **EMERGENCY PLANNING:**
   Financial networks should incorporate contingency plans for unexpected events. Financial advisors assist in crafting emergency funds and insurance strategies to mitigate financial risks during unforeseen circumstances.

Community and Collaborative Wealth-Building models emphasize collective efforts and shared resources for economic prosperity, challenging individual wealth accumulation. They involve local economic development through cooperative enterprises and partnerships, guided by financial advisors. Collaborative investing promotes informed decision-making and supportive financial networks, fostering diversified portfolios and long-term growth.

16

ADVANCED WEALTH-BUILDING STRATEGIES

John and Jane now have the normal, traditional stuff down and are ready to progress into more advanced strategies. What are some advanced wealth building strategies for them to consider?

Advanced wealth-building techniques require a thorough understanding of financial markets and go beyond conventional investing methods. A financial advisor should be consulted before beginning any advanced wealth-building strategy in order to customize strategies to the unique circumstances and risk tolerance of the investor. Here are a few advanced methods for accumulating wealth:

1. **ALTERNATIVE INVESTMENTS:**
   Diversifying a portfolio beyond stocks and bonds into alternative assets such as real estate, hedge funds, and private equity can boost returns. A financial advisor can determine whether or not these investments are appropriate based on the investor's goals and risk tolerance.

2. **TAX-EFFICIENT INVESTING:**
   Implementing tax-efficient strategies, such as tax-loss harvesting, using tax-advantaged accounts, and considering municipal bonds can minimize tax liabilities. A financial advisor can guide you through intricate tax legislation and help you make the most out of investment plans.

3. **LEVERAGE AND MARGIN TRADING:**
   Using borrowed funds to amplify investment positions can enhance returns, but it also increases risk. A financial advisor can guide investors on the prudent use of leverage, taking market conditions and individual financial situations into account.

4. **ADVANCED RETIREMENT PLANNING:**
   Beyond standard retirement accounts, high-net-worth individuals may benefit from strategies like the mega backdoor Roth IRA, non-deductible IRAs, or using life insurance as a tax-advantaged retirement vehicle. A financial advisor can devise a comprehen-

sive retirement plan incorporating these advanced elements.

5. **STRUCTURED PRODUCTS:**

   Using complex financial instruments like structured notes or derivative strategies can provide tailored risk-return profiles. A financial advisor is essential in demystifying these instruments and ensuring they align with the investor's goals.

16.1 LEGACY BUILDING THROUGH FINANCIAL WISDOM

In the pursuit of long-lasting financial success and generational prosperity, the role of a skilled financial advisor becomes paramount. Legacy building through financial wisdom involves strategic planning, prudent decision-making, and a focus on creating a lasting impact for future generations.

1. **STRATEGIC INVESTMENT PLANNING:**

   A proficient financial advisor plays a pivotal role in crafting a strategic investment plan tailored to individual goals. By leveraging market insights and considering risk tolerance, they guide clients in building a diversified portfolio that can weather economic fluctuations, ultimately contributing to the growth of family wealth.

2. **ESTATE PLANNING AND WEALTH TRANSFER:**
   Legacy building extends beyond one's lifetime, necessitating a comprehensive estate plan. Financial advisors, well-versed in tax implications and legal intricacies, assist in creating an effective wealth transfer strategy. This ensures a seamless transition of assets to heirs, minimizing tax burdens and maximizing the impact of the financial legacy.

3. **EDUCATION AND EMPOWERMENT:**
   A key aspect of financial wisdom is empowering individuals to make informed decisions regarding investments, savings, and wealth preservation. This knowledge transfer ensures that future generations are equipped to navigate the complexities of the financial landscape.

4. **PHILANTHROPIC ENDEAVORS**:
   Beyond personal wealth, financial advisors guide clients in exploring philanthropic opportunities. By incorporating charitable giving into financial plans, individuals can leave a legacy that extends beyond monetary value, contributing to societal wellbeing and leaving a positive mark on the world.

5. **ADAPTABILITY AND CONTINUOUS GUIDANCE:**
   Financial landscapes evolve, and wise legacy builders understand the importance of adaptability. Financial advisors provide ongoing

guidance, adjusting strategies as needed to align with changing economic conditions and personal circumstances, thereby safeguarding and enhancing the long-term legacy.

16.2 THE IMPORTANCE OF CONSISTENT FINANCIAL HABITS

Consistent financial habits play a pivotal role in achieving long-term financial stability and success. A disciplined approach to managing one's finances is crucial for many reasons, with the guidance of a financial advisor being particularly instrumental in this process.

1. **BUDGETING AND EXPENSE CONTROL**:
   Consistent financial habits, such as creating and adhering to a budget, help individuals track their income and expenses. This allows for better control over spending, ensuring that money is allocated wisely and unnecessary expenditures are minimized. A financial advisor can assist in developing a customized budget that aligns with an individual's financial goals.

2. **SAVINGS AND EMERGENCY FUNDS**:
   Establishing a habit of regular saving is key to building a financial cushion and preparing for unexpected expenses. A financial advisor

can provide insights into suitable savings strategies and assist in setting up emergency funds, ensuring financial resilience in the face of unforeseen challenges.

3. **DEBT MANAGEMENT**:

   Consistent financial habits also involve responsible debt management. A financial advisor can help prioritize and pay off debts strategically, preventing the accumulation of high-interest payments and fostering a healthier financial position.

4. **INVESTMENT PLANNING**:

   Investing consistently is fundamental to wealth accumulation and achieving financial goals. A financial advisor plays a crucial role in identifying suitable investment opportunities, crafting a diversified portfolio, and guiding long-term investment strategies aligned with an individual's risk tolerance and objectives.

5. **RETIREMENT PLANNING**:

   Regular contributions to retirement accounts are essential for a secure financial future. A financial advisor can assess individual retirement needs, recommend appropriate retirement plans, and ensure a consistent savings approach to meet long-term retirement goals.

16.3 DAILY, WEEKLY, AND MONTHLY FINANCIAL ROUTINES

DAILY FINANCIAL ROUTINE:

- **CHECK ACCOUNT BALANCES:** Begin each day by reviewing your bank account balances. This keeps you aware of your current financial standing and helps identify any unusual transactions.
- **EXPENSE TRACKING:** Record daily expenses in a budgeting app or spreadsheet. This habit fosters financial awareness and aids in sticking to your budget.
- **REVIEW INVESTMENTS:** If you have investments, check their performance daily. Keeping an eye on market trends ensures you can make timely adjustments with the guidance of your financial advisor.

WEEKLY FINANCIAL ROUTINE:

- **BUDGET REVIEW:** Take time each week to assess your spending against your budget. Adjust as needed and discuss any concerns or adjustments with your financial advisor.
- **DEBT CHECK:** Monitor outstanding debts and progress on repayment plans. Discuss strategies for optimizing debt management with your financial advisor to accelerate the process.

- **SAVINGS UPDATE:** Review your progress toward savings goals. Your financial advisor can suggest adjustments to ensure you're on track for both short-term and long-term objectives.

MONTHLY FINANCIAL ROUTINE:

- **INCOME AND EXPENSE ANALYSIS:** Analyze your monthly income and expenses. Identify patterns and areas for improvement with your financial advisor, who can provide insights into optimizing your cash flow.
- **INVESTMENT PORTFOLIO REVIEW:** Conduct a comprehensive review of your investment portfolio. To ensure that your investments are in line with your financial objectives, talk with your financial advisor about market trends and prospective adjustments.
- **FINANCIAL GOALS ASSESSMENT:** Assess progress towards your financial goals regularly. Whether saving for a home, education, or retirement, your financial advisor can help refine strategies to ensure you stay on the right path.

For John and Jane, advanced wealth-building entails diverse strategies beyond traditional investing, requiring a financial advisor's expertise for tailored plans. Techniques include alternative investments, tax-efficient strategies, leverage, retirement planning, and structured products. Legacy building emphasizes strategic investment planning, estate planning, education, philanthropy, and adaptability. Consistent financial habits encompass budgeting, saving, debt management, investment planning, and retirement preparation, guided by a financial advisor.

Establishing daily, weekly, and monthly financial routines includes monitoring account balances, tracking expenses, reviewing investments, budgeting, debt management, savings updates, income analysis, investment portfolio reviews, and assessing financial goals with advisor support.

CONCLUSION

This introduction to financial empowerment set the stage for a comprehensive exploration of its various dimensions and impacts. It emphasized the transformative nature of the journey toward financial empowerment, highlighting the need for self-awareness, self-control, and deliberate decision-making. The evolving global economy and changing financial landscapes underscore the urgency of financial literacy and empowerment, making them imperative in this era of shifting norms in job security and retirement strategies.

The definition of financial empowerment encompasses not only the basics of managing money, but also the development of a holistic and sustainable financial mindset. The introduction emphasized the role of financial empowerment in promoting economic equality, reducing wealth disparities, and creating resilient financial foundations capable of withstanding unforeseen challenges.

The importance of financial empowerment was explored across personal, societal, and economic dimensions. Autonomy, reduced stress, improved quality of life, entrepreneurial opportunities, and community development were among the multifaceted benefits discussed. The significance of financial empowerment in promoting gender equality, retirement planning, and crisis resilience was also underscored. The section concluded by emphasizing the transformative power of financial empowerment in shaping a more secure, dynamic, and equitable future.

The narrative proceeded to discuss the benefits of financial empowerment, highlighting its potential for improving financial stability, promoting economic mobility, lowering stress levels, and empowering underprivileged communities. The advantages extend to improved decision-making, stimulated economic growth, enhanced retirement preparedness, and resilience in times of crisis. These advantages collectively contribute to individual wellbeing and societal progress.

However, the discussion was balanced by an exploration of the potential pitfalls of financial empowerment. The acknowledgment of potential pitfalls, including exacerbation of inequality, short-term focus, risk of exploitation, emphasis on individualism, psychological stress, and the digital divide, added nuance to the narrative. This balanced perspective highlighted the importance of carefully implementing financial empowerment initiatives to avoid unintended negative consequences.

The guide then shifted focus to practical steps, starting with evaluating one's present financial condition. The importance of assessing income, expenses, debt obligations, emergency funds, investments, and financial goals was emphasized. Regular reassessment and proactive decision-making were highlighted as essential elements of navigating financial challenges successfully.

The creation of a personal financial snapshot was introduced as a crucial tool for gaining a comprehensive understanding of one's financial situation. The guide provided a step-by-step process encompassing income, expenses, net cash flow, assets, liabilities, net worth, insurance coverage, retirement savings, and financial goals. Regularly updating this snapshot was underscored as vital for effective long-term financial planning.

The income vs. expenses analysis was presented as a fundamental tool for maintaining a healthy financial equilibrium. The discussion covered income documentation, expense categorization, budgeting, savings, investments, debt management, and the importance of an emergency fund. The analysis was portrayed as a dynamic process that unveils spending patterns, identifies growth areas, and aids in decision-making for a secure financial future.

Continuing the narrative, the discussion transitioned to the pivotal aspect of income versus expenses analysis. This analysis was emphasized as a critical tool for evaluating financial health, revealing spending patterns, and guiding decisions to ensure a stable financial future.

The exploration of income covers a spectrum of earnings, from regular salaries to additional revenue streams, ensuring a thorough understanding of all financial inflows. The distinction between regular and irregular income sources was highlighted to facilitate a nuanced analysis, recognizing the dynamic nature of personal finances.

On the flip side, expenses were portrayed as financial outflows that encompassed daily expenditures, recurring bills, and debt repayments. The importance of categorizing expenses into fixed and variable was underscored, allowing individuals to discern essential costs from discretionary spending. A meticulous examination of each expense category was deemed essential to understanding where money is allocated and whether it aligns with one's financial goals.

The narrative stressed the significance of budgeting as a natural extension of the income versus expenses analysis. A well-crafted budget acts as a roadmap for financial decision-making, aligning spending with financial goals and ensuring a disciplined approach to money management.

Savings and investments were positioned as integral components of the analysis, offering insights into one's commitment to long-term financial objectives. The discussion encouraged individuals to evaluate the percentage of income devoted to savings and investments, recognizing their roles as financial safety nets and vehicles for wealth accumulation over time.

Debt management emerged as a critical facet of the analysis, delving into outstanding debts, interest rates, and their impact on overall financial health. The narrative emphasized the importance of developing a strategic approach to debt repayment, alleviating financial stress, and creating a pathway for future financial growth.

The discussion extended to the establishment and maintenance of an emergency fund, an often overlooked but crucial aspect of financial planning. The sufficiency of the emergency fund was portrayed as a key determinant of financial resilience, offering protection against unforeseen expenses and contributing to overall financial stability.

With the conclusion, the narrative underscored the dynamic nature of financial situations, necessitating regular updates and refinements. Major life events, such as marriage, the birth of a child, or career changes, were highlighted as triggers for reassessment, ensuring that financial plans remain responsive to evolving circumstances.

It has taken years, but John and Jane successfully followed their path to Financial Empowerment. This was not an overnight process. This was not an easy process, but with grit, determination, and a little bit of luck, it was a successful process. Now you too can follow these steps to Financial Empowerment and achieve what John and Jane have accomplished.

www.ingramcontent.com/pod-product-compliance
Lightning Source LLC
Chambersburg PA
CBHW071226210326
41597CB00016B/1965